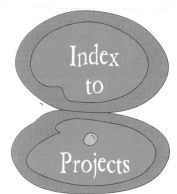

Index to Projects

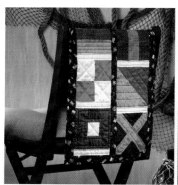

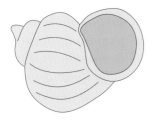

Lighthouse Table Runner
(or Chair Cover) and Pillow

Fresh as an ocean breeze, the lighthouse pillow and table runner add a maritime accent to your deck, patio, or sunroom. The bright nautical colors and inviting seaside scenery create a cheerful mood that will bring a breath of fresh ocean air to any room in your house. These applique patterns are easy to accomplish using an array of printed fabrics to achieve realistic textures.

instructions on page 23; patterns on pages 28 and 33

The lighthouse stands
so proud and tall
Its light shines
very bright.
It guards the ships
across the shoals-
Keeps sailors
safe at night.

Lighthouse Wall Hanging

Brighten up your bungalow with a wall hanging that features an artistic collection of lighthouses. Each one of these silent sentinels of the sea is unique. If you desire a smaller project, make a table runner using your favorite lighthouse design.

instructions on page 24; patterns on pages 25 - 34

Ships Flags Wall Hanging

Anchors away! The flags are up and you are welcome to take the wheel. We expect smooth sailing as we make this colorful maritime wall hanging. You'll be leaving your sewing room in your wake very quickly with this fun project. The shapes are simple, the fusible applique is easy, and the results are sure to delight every seagoing heart in your family.

instructions on pages 36 - 37; patterns on pages 38 - 41

Ships Flags Table Runner

Plan the perfect nautical picnic and deck the table with a table runner (or a chair cover) that is sure to please. Made of simple squares, this is a great beginner project that even the novice sewer will tackle with ease. Bright colors and bold solids are the secret to the success of this design.

Make it this afternoon, set it on your party table this evening!

instructions on page 35; piecing diagrams on page 37

Sailboat Pillows

When you hear the call of the sea, does your heart long for a Schooner to make the voyage? Get your first class cabin booked early on this blue sailboat with red hot sails. If your tastes run toward braving the seas alone, choose the Red Dinghy.

The patterns are so easy to assemble you won't meet any foul weather as you complete these fluffy pillows.

instructions on page 42; patterns on pages 45 and 47

Sailboat Quilt and Pillow

Got shore leave? Curl up for a cat nap in your favorite chair with this small quilt and pillow that would make any privateer or pirate envious. Let your dreams set sail for distant shores while quilted waves and clouds send you drifting into a relaxed slumber.

instructions on page 43; patterns on pages 44 - 47

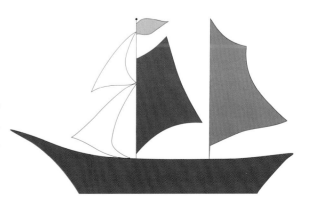

Sailboat Quilt

Wishing you calm seas and a pleasant breeze as you sail into your sewing room to make this ship-shape sailboat wall hanging. There are no hidden shoals in this easy-to-do design. Three different boat patterns are arranged in three rows to make a simply attractive quilt.

instructions on page 43; patterns on pages 44 - 47

Sailboat Table Runner

Ships Ahoy! There's a schooner off the port bow, mates! Well, actually it's hung on a chair back, or laid on the dining table, but imaginations will tend to run wild when you decorate with these colorful sailboat designs.

instructions on page 48; pattern on pages 44 - 45

Sandcastle Hanging

There is something wonderful about building sandcastles that fills a space in the soul. Welcome that feeling into your sewing room and create a castle without getting sand in your shoes. This artful design is sure to please the beach lover in every family.

instructions on page 53; patterns on pages 54 - 57

Childhood memories of the coast
With all the sounds and smells
Making castles on the beach,
Chasing waves and finding shells.

Sandcastles on the beach
Balls and pails galore
Children playing in the waves
What fun we have at the seashore.

Sand Pail Hanging

Whether you are digging for pirate gold or just playing with the beach ball in the waves, the beach is a favorite place for simple fun. Some of the best vacation times are spent where water meets the land. Your inner child will appreciate the memories that this wall hanging will bring back.

instructions on page 49; patterns on pages 50 - 52

Seaside Pillows

Take a walk along a deserted, quiet beach. It's just you and the great wide ocean. The waves are lapping at your toes. All of a sudden you look down to find a conch shell sparkling in the sand. You can't resist holding that shell to your ear. Make this daydream a little more real when you create this pretty seashell pillow. It's perfect for any room in the house.

instructions on page 60; patterns on page 61

Rubber ducky, you're so fine, and I'm so glad you are mine! These bright rubber ducks swim across a pillow. It's perfect for the nursery or a child's play room. Make this pretty pillow as a baby shower gift.

instructions on page 58; patterns on page 59

I lift a seashell to my ear
As along the beach I walk;
I listen to the ocean's sounds,
Its murmur seems to talk.

I am a rubber ducky
I love to swim in the tub
I'm yellow and I'm squeaky
And I play Rub~A~Dub~Dub!

She sells seashells
by the seashore

Clam Shells
5 cents

Snail Shells
5 cents

Scallop Shells
5 cents

Whelk Shells
5 cents

Conch Shells
10 cents

She Sells Seashells

Hand-dyed fabrics in gorgeous watercolors give character to this wall hanging that will be a favorite for the seashell hunters in your family. This simple quilt is very beautiful but easy to make.

The shell details are drawn with a pigma pen and the words were printed onto fabric with an inkjet printer.

instructions on page 64; patterns on pages 62 - 66

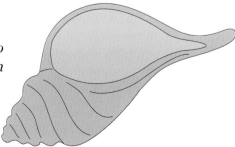

Fish Tales Hanging

"I caught a really big one, but you should have seen the one that got away! It nearly broke my pole with his pull. I tried to net it, but the net was too small." These and other fish tales have been inspired by a fetching wall hanging that will reel in more tales of lost fins than you can shake a fishing lure at. This quilt features all the sportsman's favorite things - fishing hat, creel, lures, bobs, and of course, fish! There's one on the line and that elusive one that got away.

instructions on pages 70 - 71; patterns on pages 67 - 69

Down by the Pond Hanging

Every kid loves the adventure of discovering the critters living in the pond. With its tadpoles, snails, turtle and salamander, this pond quilt is a sure way to have fun in your sewing room. Decorate your patio, porch, deck, or sunroom with this fanciful interpretation of the great outdoors. No snakes allowed unless invited by you.

This wall hanging would also be a great gift for the biology teacher or to hang in the boys' room.

instructions on page 71; patterns on pages 72 - 75

The breeze in my hair
And the sun on my face
The beach is always
My favorite place.

Breeze Hanging

Grab your sunscreen. Your favorite chair is waiting. Catch an ocean breeze in your sewing room while you make this pretty wall hanging. You'll escape to your favorite beach memory every time you look at this relaxing scene.

instructions on page 19; patterns on pages 20 - 22

Waterside
Patterns * Diagrams * Instructions

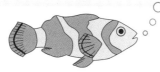

Breeze Wall Hanging

photo on page 18
patterns on pages 20 - 22
poem by Sarah Haynes Knoerr

FINISHED SIZE: 20½" x 21½"
MATERIALS:
¼ yard Blue for outer border and binding
¼ yard of the following colors: Sand, Sky, Water
⅔ yard of White for backing
For applique, scraps of Brown, Green, Grass, Shell fabrics, White, Navy, and Red • *DMC* Blue pearl cotton #5 color 311 • Black pigma pen • Steam-A-Seam II fusible web • Craft & Applique Sheet • Warm & Natural cotton batting

CUTTING:

Cut these Center strips
1   9" x 18" from Sand color
1   4" x 18" from Sky color
1   5½" x 18" from Water color

Cut out Blue Border
2 strips   2" x 17½" for sides
2 strips   2" x 21" for top and bottom

BACKING AND BATTING
1   21" x 22"

BINDING:

Cut 2" strips and sew together for 84"

INSTRUCTIONS:
1. Sew the 4" x 18" strip to the 5½" x 18" strip.
2. Sew these to the sand color 9" x 18" strip.
3. Sew the Blue 2" x 17½" strips to each side.
4. Sew the Blue 2" x 21" strips to top and bottom.
APPLIQUE:
1. Trace all of the applique pieces in reverse onto the fusible web paper using a light table.
2. Using the picture as a color guide, press the traced fusible web pieces to appropriate fabrics.
3. Cut out shapes.
4. Lay the poem pattern on the light table.

Breeze Wall Hanging Assembly Diagram

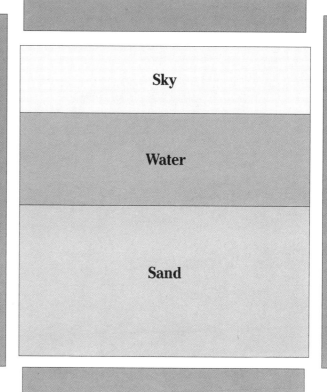

5. Lay the pieced top directly on top so you can see the poem. Trace the poem and embroider with pearl cotton using a Backstitch.
6. Peel paper backing off of each piece and position them directly on top of the pieced top as shown in photo.
7. Press with iron for 12-14 seconds.
8. Using a Black pigma pen, draw bird leg, eye, beak, and lines on shells.
9. Using pearl cotton, Backstitch lines as desired on the chair.
10. Follow the finishing instructions on page 82.

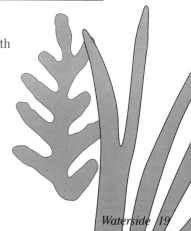

Breeze Wall Hanging
photo on page 18

Grass
Pattern

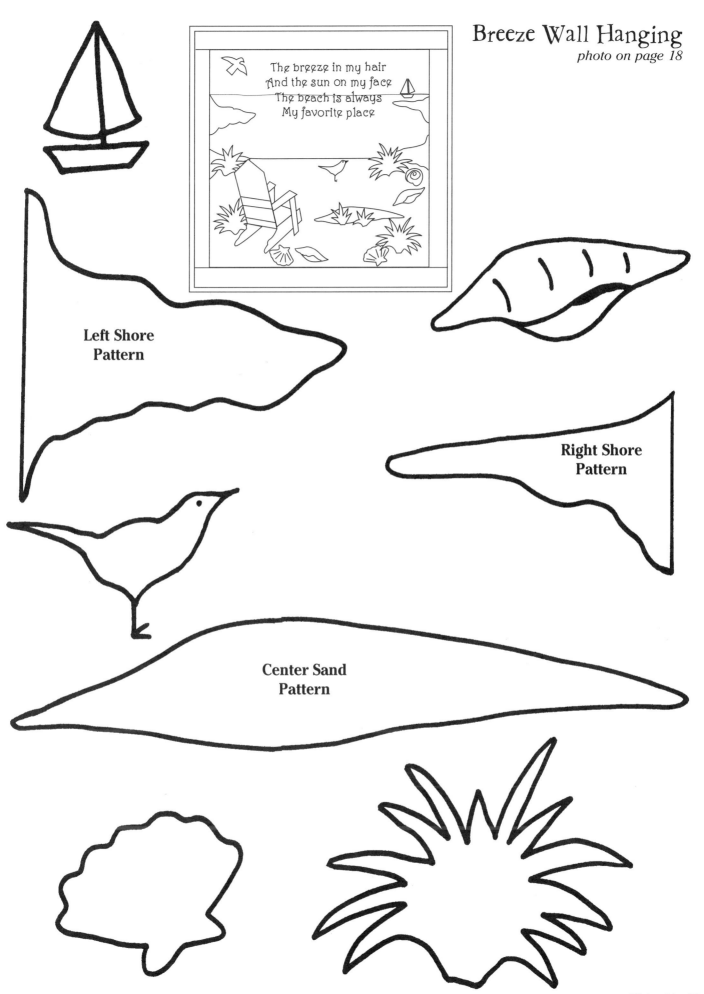

Breeze Wall Hanging
photo on page 18

The breeze in my hair
And the sun on my face
The beach is always
My favorite place

Left Shore Pattern

Right Shore Pattern

Center Sand Pattern

The breeze in my hair
And the sun on my face
The beach is always
My favorite place

Breeze Hanging
photo on page 18
poem by Sarah Haynes Knoerr

Lighthouse Table Runner

photo on page 4

pattern on page 28

FINISHED SIZE: 15½" x 32½"
MATERIALS:
⅓ yard Sky fabric for center
⅓ yard Dark Blue for border and binding
½ yard White backing fabric
For applique, ¼ yard cuts or scraps of Green, Bright Red, Dark Red, Brown wood, Sandy beach, Navy, Gray • Steam-A-Seam II fusible web • Craft & Applique Sheet • Warm & Natural cotton batting

CUTTING:
Cut out Sky Center
1   12" x 30"

Cut out Blue Borders
2 strips   2" x 30" for sides
2 strips   2" x 15" for top and bottom

BACKING AND BATTING
1   16" x 33"

BINDING:
Cut 2" strips and sew together for 100"

Table Runner

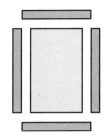

INSTRUCTIONS:

1. Sew a 2" x 30" border to each side of the center panel.
2. Sew a 2" x 15" border strip to the top and bottom.

APPLIQUE:

1. Using pattern for Lighthouse #4 on page 28, trace 2 sets of all of the applique pieces in reverse onto the fusible web paper.
2. Using the picture as a color guide, press the traced fusible web pieces to the appropriate fabrics.
3. Cut out shapes.
4. Lay the paper pattern on the ironing board. Lay the Craft & Applique Sheet directly on top so you can see through to the pattern. Peel paper backing off of each piece and lay them directly on top of the Craft & Applique Sheet over the pattern. Press for 2-4 seconds. Cool completely.
5. Peel the lighthouse shape off of the Craft & Applique Sheet and position on 1 end of the table runner. Repeat for other end.
6. Once both lighthouses are in place, press with iron for 12-14 seconds.
7. Sew binding strips end to end to make a continuous strip.
8. Follow Finishing instructions on page 82.

Lighthouse Pillow

photo on page 4
pattern on page 33

FINISHED SIZE: 13½" x 16½"

MATERIALS:

⅓ yard of Blue sky for center block
¼ yard of Navy Blue for inner border
½ yard Red polka dot print for outer border and pillow back
For applique, ¼ yard cuts or scraps of Red, Black, White, Sand, Gray, Green, Dark Red • Steam-A-Seam II fusible web • Craft & Applique Sheet • Warm & Natural cotton batting • Poly-fil stuffing

CUTTING:

Cut out Blue Sky Center
1   9" x 12"

Cut out Navy Blue Inner Border
2 strips   1½" x 12" for sides
2 strips   1½" x 11" for top and bottom

Cut out Red Outer Border

2 strips   2" x 14" for sides
2 strips   2" x 14" for top and bottom

Cut out Red Pillow Back
1   14" x 17"

Cut out batting squares
2   14" x 17"

Pillow Assembly

1. Making Center Block.

2. Add second border.

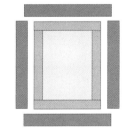

INSTRUCTIONS:

1. Sew a 1½" x 12" Navy strip to each side of the center block.
2. Sew a 1½" x 11" strip to the top and bottom.
3. Sew a 2" x 14" Red strip to each side.
4. Sew a 2" x 14" Red strip to the top and bottom.

APPLIQUE:

1. Using pattern for Lighthouse #8 on page 33, trace all of the applique pieces in reverse onto the fusible web paper.
2. Using the picture as a color guide, press the traced fusible web pieces to the appropriate fabrics.
3. Cut out shapes.
4. Lay the paper pattern on the ironing board. Lay the Craft & Applique Sheet directly on top so you can see through to the pattern. Peel paper backing off of each piece and lay them directly on top of the Craft & Applique Sheet over the pattern. Press for 2-4 seconds. Cool completely.
5. Peel the lighthouse shape off of the Craft & Applique Sheet and position on the pillow top. Once the lighthouse is in place, press with iron for 12-14 seconds.
6. Follow Pillow instructions on page 82 to finish.

Lighthouse
Wall Hanging

photo on page 5
patterns on pages 25 - 34
poem by Sarah Haynes Knoerr

FINISHED SIZE: 36½" x 43½"
MATERIALS:
1⅛ yards Blue Sky background
¾ yard Dark Blue for border, sashing, and binding
1¼ yard White backing fabric

For applique, ¼ yard cuts or scraps of White, Black, Gray, Brown, Dark Red, Bright Red, Red Stripe, Brown and Gray roof fabric, several shades of Green, Tan grass print, Rock print for lighthouse, Brick print for chimneys • *DMC* pearl cotton #5 color 823 for words • Black Pigma pen • Steam-A-Seam II fusible web • Craft & Applique Sheet • Warm & Natural cotton batting

CUTTING:

Cut out Blue Sky backgrounds
2   9½" x 12½" for Blocks 1 and 8
2   11½" x 12½" for Blocks 2 and 9
2   10½" x 12½" for Blocks 3 and 7
3   10½" x 13½" for Blocks 4, 5, and 6

Cut out Dark Blue Sashings
2 strips   1½" x 32½"
4 strips   1½" x 12½" for rows 1 & 3
2 strips   1½" x 13½" for row 2

Cut out Dark Blue Borders
2 strips   2½" x 39½" for sides
2 strips   2½" x 36½" for top and bottom

BACKING AND BATTING:
1   37½" x 44½"

BINDING:
Cut 2" strips and sew together for 164"

APPLIQUE:

1. Trace all of the applique pieces in reverse onto the fusible web paper using a light table.
2. Using each picture as a color guide, press the traced fusible web pieces to the appropriate fabrics.
3. Cut out shapes.
4. Lay the paper pattern on the ironing board. Lay the Craft & Applique Sheet directly on top so you can see thru to the pattern. Peel paper backing off of each piece and lay them directly on top of the Craft & Applique Sheet over the pattern. Press for 2-4 seconds. Cool completely.
5. Press each lighthouse shape off of the Craft & Applique Sheet and position onto the appropriate quilt block.
6. Once the lighthouses are all in place, press with iron for 12-14 seconds.
7. Sew the binding strips together end to end to make a continuous strip for binding.
8. Follow Finishing instructions on page 82.

The lighthouse stands
so proud and tall
Its light shines
very bright.
It guards the ships
across the shoals-
Keeps sailors
safe at night.

INSTRUCTIONS:
ROW 1
1. Sew a 1½" x 12½" sashing strip to each side of Block 2.
2. Sew Block 1 to the left side.
3. Sew Block 3 to the right side.
4. Sew a 1½" x 32½" sashing piece to the bottom of row 1.
ROW 2
1. Sew a 1½" x 13½" sashing strip to each side of Block 5.
2. Sew Block 4 to the left side.
3. Sew Block 6 to the right side.
4. Sew a 1½" x 32½" sashing strip to the bottom of row 2.
5. Sew row 2 to the bottom of row 1.
ROW 3
1. Sew a 1½" x 12½" sashing strip to each side of block 8.
2. Sew block 7 to the left side.
3. Sew block 9 to the right side.
4. Sew this row to the bottom of row 2.
5. Sew the 2½" x 39½" border strips to each side.
6. Sew the 2½" x 36½" border strips to the top and bottom.
EMBROIDERY:
1. Using a light table, trace the poem centered on Block 5.
2. Using a Backstitch, embroider the words with *DMC* pearl cotton #823.

Lighthouse Wall Hanging Block Assembly

Lighthouse Wall Hanging Border Assembly

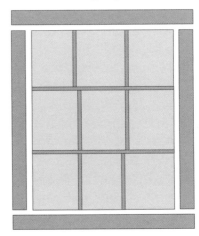

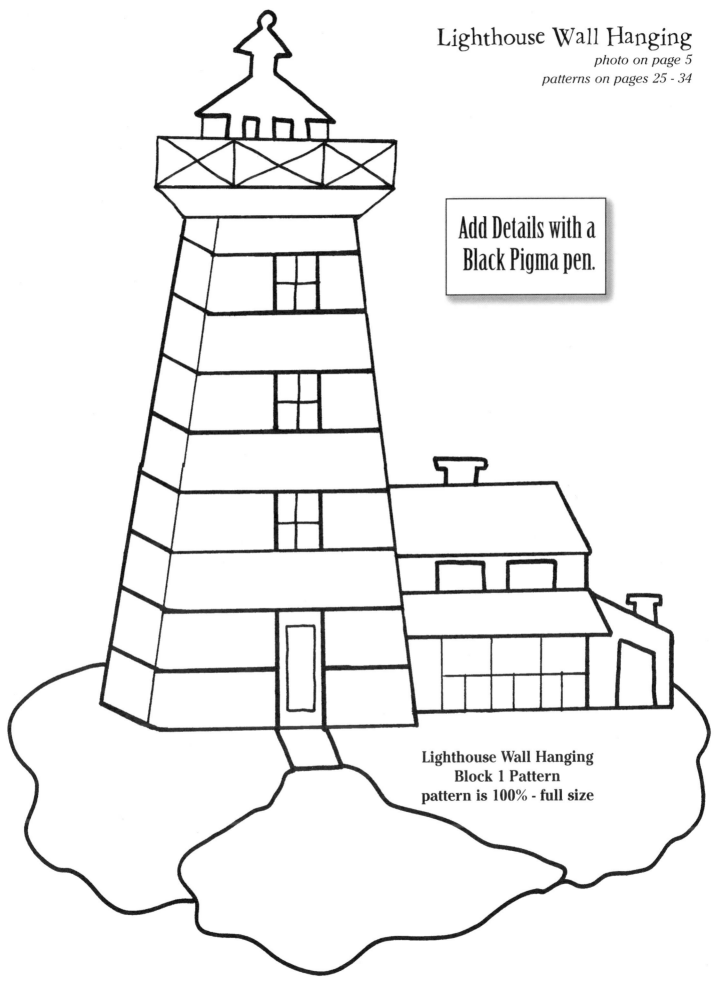

Lighthouse Wall Hanging
photo on page 5
patterns on pages 25 - 34

Add Details with a
Black Pigma pen.

Lighthouse Wall Hanging
Block 1 Pattern
pattern is 100% - full size

Lighthouse Wall Hanging

photo on page 5
patterns on pages 25 - 34

The lighthouse stands
so proud and tall
Its light shines
very bright.
It guards the ships
across the shoals-
Keeps sailors
safe at night.

Add Details with a Black Pigma pen.

**Lighthouse Wall Hanging
Block 2 Pattern
enlarge pattern 140%**

Add Details with a
Black Pigma pen.

Lighthouse Wall Hanging
Block 3 Pattern
enlarge pattern 140%

Lighthouse Wall Hanging and Table Runner

photos on pages 5 & 45
patterns on pages 25 - 34

Add Details with a
Black Pigma pen.

Lighthouse
Wall Hanging

Block 4
Pattern

enlarge
pattern 140%

Lighthouse Wall Hanging

photo on page 5
patterns on pages 25 - 34

The lighthouse stands
so proud and tall
Its light shines
very bright.
It guards the ships
across the shoals-
Keeps sailors
safe at night.

Add Details with a Black Pigma pen.

Lighthouse Wall Hanging Block 6 Pattern enlarge pattern 140%

Lighthouse
Wall
Hanging

photo on page 5
patterns on pages
25 - 34
poem by
Sarah Haynes Knoerr

Lighthouse
Wall Hanging

Embroider Words
on Block 5

The lighthouse stands

so proud and tall

Its light shines

very bright.

Lighthouse
Wall Hanging
photo on page 5
patterns on pages 25 - 34
poem by Sarah Haynes Knoerr

It guards the ships
across the shoals~

Keeps sailors
safe at night.

Lighthouse Wall Hanging

photo on page 5
patterns on pages 25 - 34

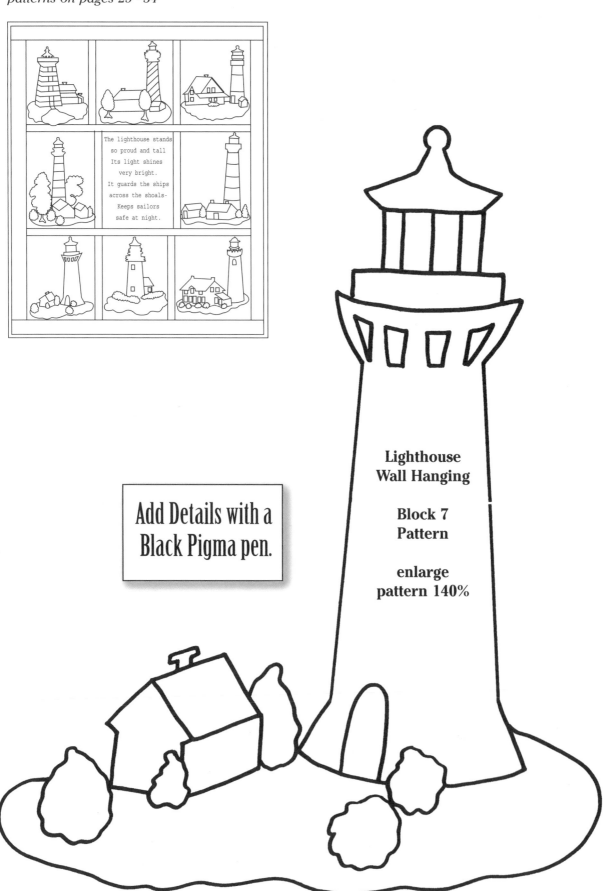

The lighthouse stands
so proud and tall
Its light shines
very bright.
It guards the ships
across the shoals-
Keeps sailors
safe at night.

Add Details with a Black Pigma pen.

Lighthouse Wall Hanging

Block 7 Pattern

enlarge pattern 140%

Add Details with a Black Pigma pen.

**Lighthouse Wall Hanging
Block 8 Pattern
enlarge pattern 140%**

Lighthouse
Wall Hanging

photo on page 5
patterns on pages 25 - 34

The lighthouse stands
so proud and tall
Its light shines
very bright.
It guards the ships
across the shoals-
Keeps sailors
safe at night.

Add Details with a
Black Pigma pen.

Lighthouse
Wall Hanging

Block 9
Pattern

enlarge
pattern 140%

Ships Flags
Table Runner

photo on page 7
piecing diagrams on page 37

FINISHED SIZE: 16" x 38"
MATERIALS:
⅓ yard Nautical print for border and binding
½ yard White for backing
¼ yard cuts of the following for pieced blocks: Navy Blue, Navy Stripe, Medium Dark Blue, Gold Stripe, Bright Red, Red Polka Dot, Red Stripe, Cream

CUTTING:

Cut out from Navy Blue
1   6½" square for G
2   3¼" square for E
1   2½" square for B
Cut out from Navy Blue Stripe
2   2½" squares for J
2   2½" x 6½" strips for J
2   3½" squares for A
Cut out from Medium Dark
    Blue
2   2½" x 6½" strips for C
Cut out from Gold Stripe
2   2½" squares for B
2   2½" x 6½" strips for B
1   6½" square for D
Cut out from Gold
2   2½" x 6½" strips for H
1   2" x 8½" strip for E
2   2" x 4" strips for E
Cut out from Bright Red
2   3½" squares for I
3   2½" x 6½" strips for F
1   2½" x 6½" strips for C

Cut out from Red Polka Dot
1   6½" square for D
Cut out from Red Stripe
1   2½" x 6½" strips for H
Cut out from Cream
1   6½" square for G
4   3½" squares for A and I
1   2½" x 6½" strip for F
1   2½" square for J
10   1½" x 6½" strips
Cut out from Nautical print for
    Border
3 strips   1½" x 35½" for sides
    and middle
2 strips   1½" x 15½" for top
and bottom

BACKING AND BATTING:
1   16½" x 38½"

BINDING:
Cut 2" strips and sew together
for 110"

INSTRUCTIONS:

Row 1:
Block A: See Block Assembly diagram on page 37.
1. Sew each 3½" Cream square to a 3½" Navy Stripe square.
2. Alternate the colors and sew the 2 rows together.
3. Sew a 1½" x 6½" Cream strip to one side.
Block B: See Block Assembly diagram on page 37.
1. Sew a 2½" Gold Stripe square to 2 sides of the 2½" Navy Blue square.
2. Sew a 2½" x 6½" Gold Stripe to each 6½" side.
3. Sew a 1½" x 6½" Cream strip to each side.
Block C: See Block Assembly diagram on page 37.
1. Sew a 2½" x 6½" Medium Dark Blue strip to each side of a 2½" x 6½" Bright Red strip.
Block D: See Block Assembly diagram on page 37.
1. With right sides together, sew the 6½" Red Polka Dot square to the 6½" Gold Stripe square diagonally through the center.
2. Cut ¼" away from the seam. Set the leftover pieces aside.
3. Open the seam and press flat.
4. Sew a 1½" x 6½" Cream strip to each side.
Block E: See Block Assembly diagram K on page 37.
1. Cut the 3¼" Navy Blue squares in half diagonally.
2. Sew the 2" x 4" Gold strip to each side.
3. Sew the 2" x 8½" Gold strip to each long side.
4. Trim the corners to measure 6½" square.
5. Referring to diagram, sew Blocks A thru E together.

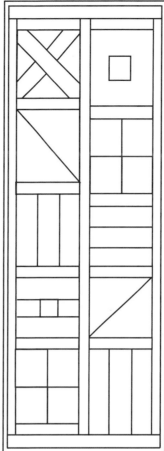

Row 2:
Block F: See Block Assembly diagram C on page 37.
1. Sew a 2½" x 6½" Bright Red strip to each side of a 2½" x 6½" Cream strip.
2. Sew the 1½" x 6½" Cream strip to the right side.
Block G: See Block Assembly diagram D on page 37.
1. With right sides together, sew the 6½" Navy Blue square to the 6½" Cream square diagonally through the center.
2. Cut ¼" away from the seam. Set the leftover pieces aside.
3. Open the seam and press flat.
Block H: See Block Assembly diagram C on page 37.
1. Sew a 2½" x 6½" Gold strip to each side of a 2½" x 6½" Red Stripe.
2. Sew the 1½" x 6½" Cream strip to each side.
Block I: See Block Assembly diagram A on page 37.
1. Sew each 3½" Cream square to each 3½" Bright Red square.
2. Alternate the colors and sew the 2 rows together.
Block J: See Block Assembly diagram B on page 37.
1. Sew a 2½" Navy Stripe square to 2 sides of the 2½" Cream square.
2. Sew a 2½" x 6½" Navy Stripe to each side of this.
3. Sew the 1½" x 6½" Cream strip to each side.
Referring to diagram, sew Blocks F thru J together.
Sashing and Borders:
1. Sew 1½" x 35½" border fabric strip to the right side of Row 1.
2. Sew Row 2 to the other side of the sashing.
3. Sew a 1½" x 35½" border fabric strip to each side.
4. Sew a 1½" x 15½"" border fabric strip to each end.
5. Sew the binding pieces together, end to end, to make a continuous strip.
6. Follow Finishing instructions on page 82.

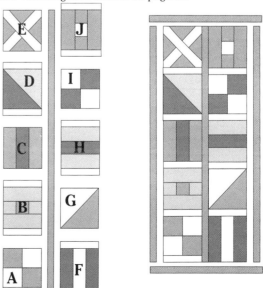

Flag Ship Table Runner Block & Border Assembly

Ships Flags
Wall Hanging

photo on page 6
patterns on pages 38 - 41

FINISHED SIZE: 32" x 35"
MATERIALS:
⅓ yard Cream for center panel
¼ yard Dark Red for sashing
½ yard Dark Red print for border and binding
l yard White backing fabric
For applique, ¼ yard cuts or scraps of Cream, Navy stripe, Navy Blue, Medium Dark Blue, Bright Red, Red Polka Dot, Red Plaid, Gold, Gold Stripe, Brown, Gray, White • Steam-A-Seam II fusible web
• Craft & Applique Sheet
• Warm & Natural cotton batting

CUTTING:

Cut out from Cream
1   10½" square for center panel
6   1½" x 6½" strips for A, C, and J
2   3½" squares for A

Cut out from Navy Stripe
2   8½" x 10½" blocks for E and G

Cut out from Navy Blue
2   6½" x 7½" blocks for I and L
1   2½" square for B

Cut out from Medium Dark Blue
1   6½" x 28½" strip for H
1   6½" square for D
2   3¼" squares for K

Cut out from Red Polka Dot fabric
2   2½" x 6½" strips for C and J

Cut out from Bright Red fabric
2   3½" squares for A

Cut out from Gold
2   2½" x 6½" strips for B
2   2½" squares for B
1   6½" square for D
1   2" x 8½" strip for K
2   2" x 4" strips for K

Cut out from Gold Stripe
2   2½" x 6½" strips for J

Cut out from Red Sashing
3 strips   1½" x 28½" for horizontal sashing
2 strips   1½" x 10½" for vertical sashing

Cut out from Dark Red print for Border
2 strips   2½" x 31½" for sides
2 strips   2½" x 32½" for top and bottom

BACKING AND BATTING
1   33" x 36"

BINDING:
Cut 2" strips and sew together for 138"

1. Cut out all the blocks, sashing and border strips.
Row 1: Block A: See Block Assembly diagram.
1. Sew a 3½" Cream square to a 3½" Bright Red square.
2. Repeat for the other two squares.
3. Alternate the colors and sew the four squares together.
4. Sew a Cream 1½" x 6½" strip to each side.
Block B: See Block Assembly diagram.
1. Sew a 2½" Gold square to two sides of the 2½" Navy square.
2. Sew a 2½" x 6½" Gold strip to each 6½" side.
3. Sew to the right side of Block A.
Block C: See Block Assembly diagram.
1. Sew a 2½" x 6½" Cream strip to each long side of a 2½" x 6½" Red Polka Dot strip.
2. Sew a 1½" x 6½" Cream strip to each side.
3. Sew to the right side of Block B.
Block D: See Block Assembly diagram.
1. With right sides together, sew the 6½" Gold square to the 6½" Medium Blue square diagonally through the center. Cut ¼" away from the seam. Set the left-over pieces aside.
2. Open the seam and press flat.
3. Sew to the right side of Block C.
4. Sew a 1½" x 28½" sashing to the bottom of row 1.
Row 2: 1. Sew 1½" x 10½" sashing to right side of Block E.
2. Sew this to Block F.
3. Sew the other 1½" x 10½" sashing to the right side of block F.
4. Sew block G to the right side of the sashing.
5. Sew a 1½" x 28½" sashing to the bottom.
Row 3: 1. Sew remaining 1½" x 28½" sashing to bottom of block H.
Row 4: Block I:
1. Sew the 1½" x 6½" Cream strip to the right side of Block I.
Block J: See Block Assembly diagram.
1. Sew a 2½" x 6½" Gold strip to each side of the 2½" x 6½" Red Polka Dot strip.
2. Sew a 1½" x 6½" Cream strip to the right side.
3. Sew Block J to the right side of Block I.
Block K: See Block Assembly diagram.
1. Cut the 2 Medium Dark Blue 3¼" squares in half diagonally to make four triangles.
2. Sew one triangle to each side of the 2" x 4" Gold strip.
3. Sew the 2" x 8½" strip across top of the triangle.
4. Add the other side.
5. Trim corners to measure 6½" square
6. Sew to Block J.
Block L: 1. Sew Block L to the right side of this row.

Ships Flags Wall Hanging

photo on page 6
patterns on pages 38 - 41

Ships Flags Wall Hanging Block Assembly

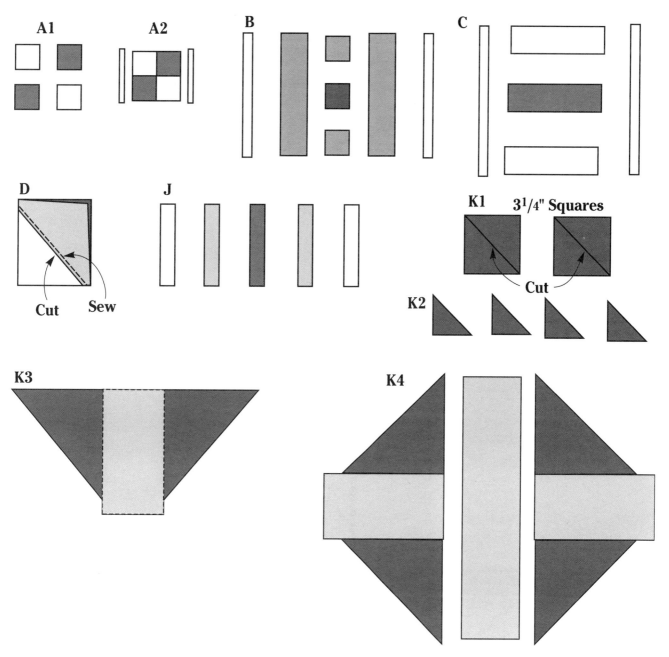

INSTRUCTIONS:

ASSEMBLY:

1. Sew Row 1 to Row 2.
2. Add Rows 3 and 4.
3. Sew the 2½" x 31½" border strips to each side.
4. Sew the 2½" x 32½" border strips to the top and bottom.

APPLIQUE:

1. Trace all of the applique pieces in reverse onto the fusible web paper using a light table.
2. Using the picture as a color guide, press the traced fusible web pieces to the appropriate fabrics.

3. Cut out shapes.
4. Peel off backing and position pieces.
5. Lay the paper pattern on the ironing board. Lay the Craft & Applique Sheet directly on top so you can see through to the pattern. Peel paper backing off of each piece and lay them directly on top of the Craft & Applique Sheet over the pattern. Press for 2-4 seconds. Cool completely.
6. Peel the shape off of the Craft & Applique Sheet and position on the quilt. Press with iron for 12-14 seconds.
7. Sew binding strips together, end to end, to make one continuous strip for the binding.
8. Follow Finishing instructions on page 82.

Ships Flags Wall Hanging

photo on page 6
patterns on pages 38 - 41

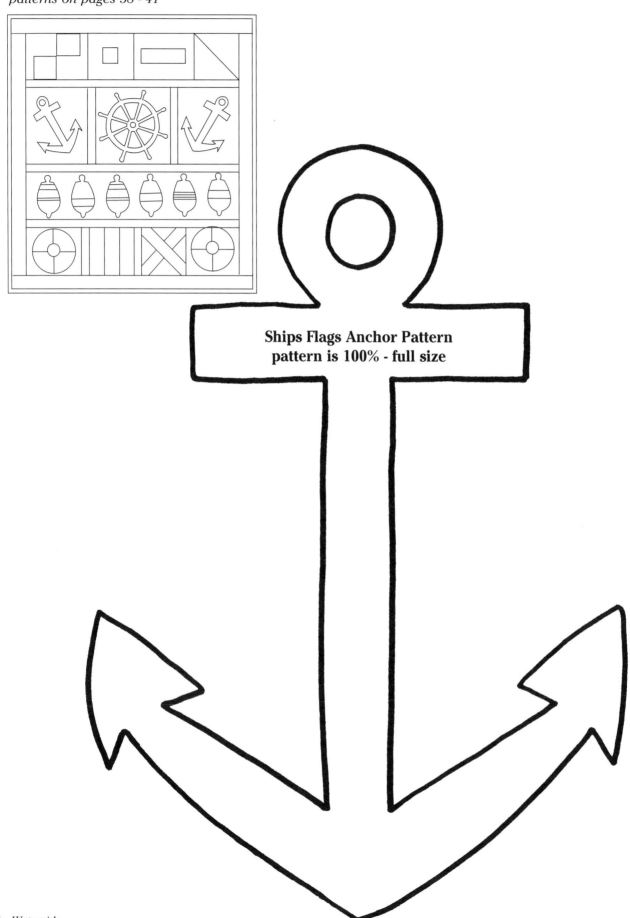

Ships Flags Anchor Pattern
pattern is 100% - full size

Ships Flags Wall Hanging

photo on page 6
patterns on pages 38 - 41

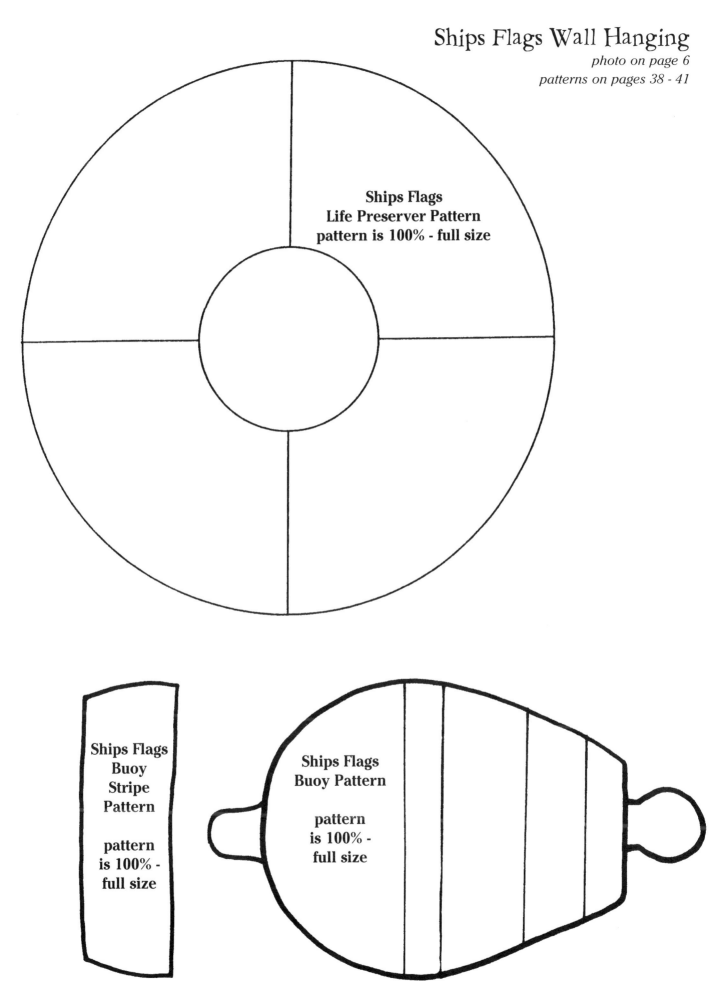

**Ships Flags
Life Preserver Pattern
pattern is 100% - full size**

**Ships Flags
Buoy
Stripe
Pattern**

**pattern
is 100% -
full size**

**Ships Flags
Buoy Pattern**

**pattern
is 100% -
full size**

Ships Flags Wall Hanging

photo on page 6
patterns on pages 38 - 41

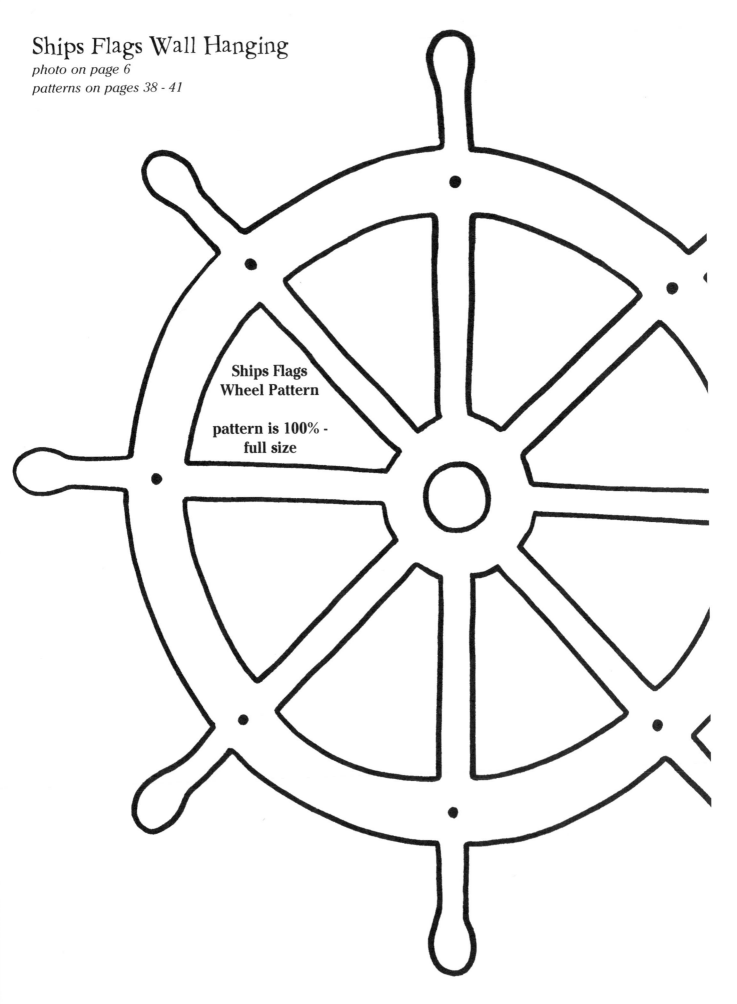

**Ships Flags
Wheel Pattern**

**pattern is 100% -
full size**

Ships Flags Wall Hanging

photo on page 6
patterns on pages 38 - 41

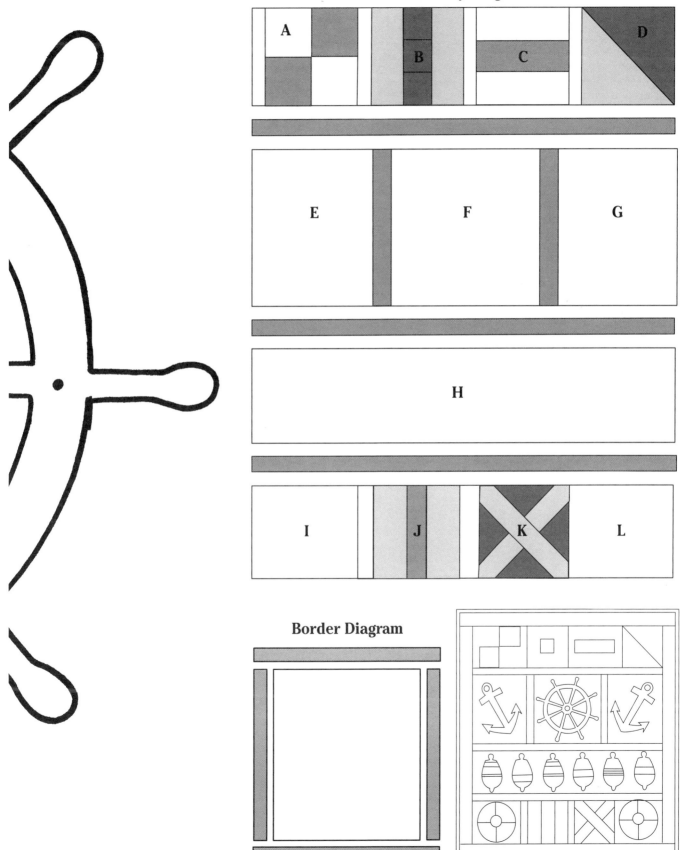

Assembly Diagram

A   B   C   D

E   F   G

H

I   J   K   L

Border Diagram

Sailboat Pillows

photo on page 8
pattern on page 47

Red Dinghy Pillow

photo on page 8
pattern on page 45

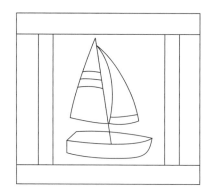

FINISHED SIZE: 17" x 17"
MATERIALS:
⅓ yard Blue Ocean fabric for center panel
⅛ yard Red for inner border
½ yard Navy Blue for border and backing
For applique, ¼ yard cuts or scraps of Navy, Red, White • *DMC* Brown pearl cotton #5 • Steam-A-Seam II fusible web • Craft & Applique Sheet • Warm & Natural cotton batting • Poly-fil stuffing

CUTTING:

Cut out Blue Ocean Center block
1   10½" x 12½"

Cut out Red Inner Border
2 strips   1½" x 12½" for sides

Cut out Navy Outer Border
2 strips   3" x 12½" for sides
2 strips   3" x 17½" for top and bottom

Cut out Navy Backing
1   17½" x 17½"

Cut out batting
2   17½" x 17½"

INSTRUCTIONS:

1. Sew the 1½" x 12½" Red strips to each side of the center block.
2. Sew the 3" x 12½" Navy strips to each side of the Red strips.
3. Sew the 3" x 17½" Navy strips to the top and bottom.

APPLIQUE:

1. Trace the Red Dinghy pattern pieces in reverse on the fusible web paper.
2. Press each piece to Red, Navy, and White and cut out pieces. Remove paper backing.
3. Using a light table, assemble the boat onto the center square and press in place.
4. Backstitch boat mast with Brown pearl cotton.
5. Follow Pillow instructions on page 82.

Red Dinghy Pillow Assembly

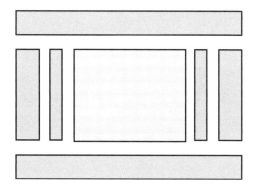

Blue Schooner Pillow

photo on page 8
pattern on pages 46 - 47

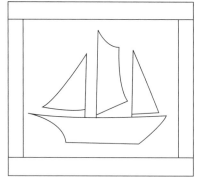

FINISHED SIZE: 17" x 19"
MATERIALS:
½ yard Blue Ocean fabric for center panel
½ yard Dark Red Buoy print for border and backing
For applique, ¼ yard cuts or scraps of Navy, Red • *DMC* Brown pearl cotton #5 • Steam-A-Seam II fusible web • Craft & Applique Sheet • Warm & Natural cotton batting • Poly-fil stuffing

INSTRUCTIONS:

1. Sew a 3" x 12½" Dark Red strip to each side of the center block.
2. Sew the 3" x 19½" Dark Red strip to the top and bottom of the center block.
APPLIQUE:

1. Trace Triple Masted Schooner pattern pieces in reverse on the fusible web paper.
2. Press each piece to Red and Navy and cut out pieces. Remove paper backing.
3. Using a light table, assemble boat onto the pillow top and press in place.
4. Backstitch boat masts with Brown pearl cotton.
5. Follow Pillow instructions on page 82.

CUTTING:

Cut out Blue Ocean Center block
1   12½" x 14½"

Cut out Dark Red Border
2 strips   3" x 12½" for sides
2 strips   3" x 19½" for top and bottom

Cut out Rust pillow back
1   17½" x 19½"

Cut out batting
2   17½" x 19½"

Blue Schooner Pillow Assembly

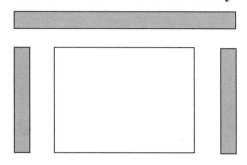

Sailboat Quilt

photo on page 10
diagrams on pages 43 - 44;
patterns on pages 44 - 47

FINISHED SIZE: 45" x 47"

MATERIALS:

1 yard Blue Sky/Water fabric

¼ yard Dark Navy Blue for sashing and applique

½ yard Brick Red print for border and binding (If you choose a directional or 1-way print, you will need more fabric.)

3 yards White backing fabric

For applique, ¼ yard cuts or scraps of Navy Blue print, Dark Red, Bright Red, 2 shades Red Stripe, Red Polka Dot, Red Plaid, Gold, 2 shades Gold stripe • *DMC* Brown pearl cotton #5 • Steam-A-Seam II fusible web • Craft & Applique Sheet • Warm & Natural cotton batting

CUTTING:

Cut out BLOCKS from Blue Sky/Water

3	10½" x 14½"	for A
3	12½" x 14½"	for B
3	10½" x 12½"	for C

Cut out Bright Red strips for Block A
3 strips   2½" x 14½"

Cut out Dark Red strips for Block C
2 strips   2½" x 12½"

Cut out Dark Navy Blue strips
4 strips   2½" x 12½" (for Block C)
2 strips   2½" x 42½"

Cut out from Brick Red print BORDER fabric:
2 strips   2½" x 40½" for sides
3 strips   2½" x 44" for top and bottom - These will need to be pieced to make 2 strips 2½" x 46½".

BACKING AND BATTING
1   45½" x 47½"

BINDING:

Cut 2" strips and sew together for 188"

INSTRUCTIONS:

1. Cut out all the blocks, strips and borders.
Block Assembly: See diagrams on pages 44 - 45.
Block A:
1. For Row 1, sew a 2½" x 14½" Red strip to the top of the 10½" x 14½" Sky block.
2. For Rows 2 and 3, sew a 2½" x 14½" Red strip to the bottom of the 10½" x 14½" Sky block.
Block B:
1. This block is just a 12½" x 14½" Sky block.
2. Make sure you cut 3.
Block C:
1. For Rows 1 and 3, sew a 2½" x 12½" Navy Blue strip to each side of the 10½" x 12½" Sky block.
2. For Row 2, sew a 2½" x 12½" Dark Red strip to each side of the 10½" x 12½" Sky block.

ROW ASSEMBLY:

See diagrams on page 45.
1. **Row 1**: Sew blocks A, B, and C together.
2. Sew a 2½" x 42½" Dark Navy Blue strip to the bottom of Row 1.
3. **Row 2**: Sew blocks B, C, and A together.
4. Sew a 2½" x 42½" Dark Navy Blue strip to the bottom of Row 2.
5. Sew Row 2 to bottom of Row 1.
6. **Row 3**: Sew blocks C, A, and B together.
7. Sew to the bottom of Row 2.
Borders: See diagrams on page 45.
8. Sew a 2½" x 40½" Brick Red print strip to each side.
9. Sew a 2½" x 46½" Brick Red print strip to the top and bottom.

APPLIQUE:

1. Patterns for Block A on page 44. Patterns for Block B on pages 46 - 47. Patterns for Block C on page 45.
2. Trace the boat pattern pieces in reverse on the fusible web paper for each block.
3. Press each piece to the appropriate fabrics and cut out pieces. Remove backing.
4. Using a light table, assemble each boat and press in place.
5. Backstitch the masts with Brown pearl cotton #5 as shown in picture.
6. Sew the binding strips together to make 188".
7. Follow the Finishing instructions on page 82.

Sailboat Quilt Blocks A & C Assembly

Row 1: A   **Rows: A2 & 3**   **Rows: C1 & 3**

Row: C2

Continued on page 44

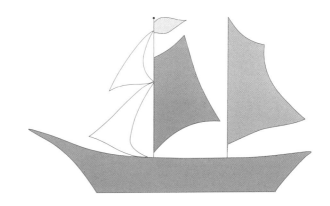

Sailboat Quilt

photo on page 10
diagrams on page 44; patterns on pages 45 - 47

Row Assembly

Border Assembly

Double-Masted Ship Pattern
enlarge pattern 140%

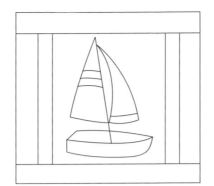

Sailboat Quilt &
Red Dinghy Pillow

photo on page 10
diagrams on page 44; patterns on
pages 45 - 47

**Sailboat Quilt
and
Red Dinghy
Pillow Pattern**

enlarge pattern 140%

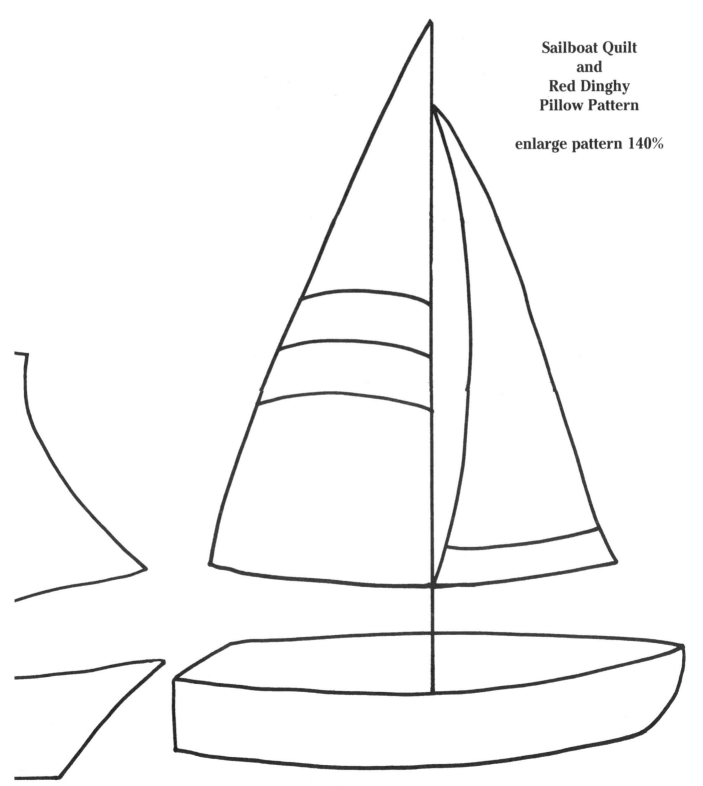

Sailboat Quilt

photo on pages 8 - 10
diagrams on page 44; patterns on pages 45 - 47

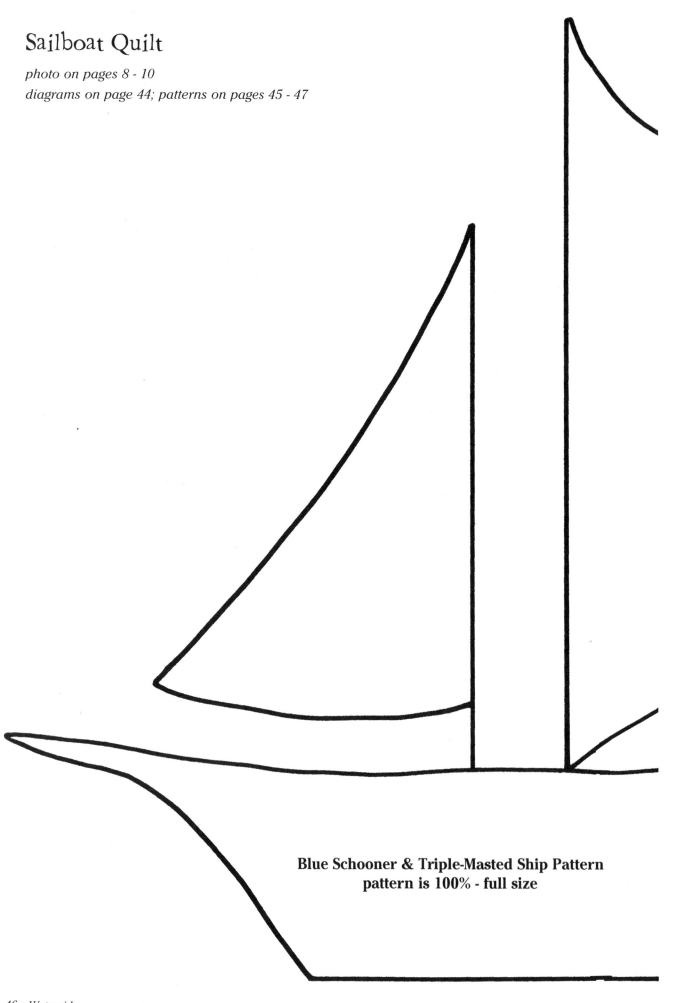

**Blue Schooner & Triple-Masted Ship Pattern
pattern is 100% - full size**

Sailboat Table Runner

photo on page 11

pattern on pages 44 - 45

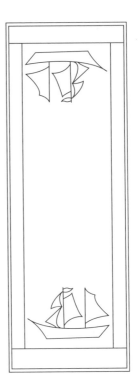

FINISHED SIZE: 15½" x 36½"

MATERIALS:

½ yard Blue Sky fabric

¼ yard Blue Ocean fabric

⅓ yard Navy Blue for border and binding

½ yard White backing fabric

For applique, ¼ yard cuts or scraps of Navy, Red, Gold, White • *DMC* Brown pearl cotton #5 • Steam-A-Seam II fusible web • Craft & Applique Sheet • Warm & Natural cotton batting

CUTTING:

Cut out Blue Sky Center Block

1   13½" x 18½"

Cut out Blue Ocean End Blocks

2   8½" x 13½"

Cut out Navy Blue Border

2 strips   1½" x 34½" for sides

2 strips   1½" x 15½" for ends

BACKING AND BATTING

1   16½" x 37½"

BINDING:

Cut 2" strips and sew together for 106"

INSTRUCTIONS:

1. Sew the 8½" x 13½" water panels to each end of the center sky fabric.
2. Sew the 1½" x 34½" side borders to each side.
3. Sew the 1½" x 15½" strips to each end.
4. Sew the binding pieces together, end to end, to make a continuous strip for binding.

APPLIQUE:

1. Trace two sets of the Double Masted Sailboat pattern pieces in reverse on the fusible web paper.
2. Press each piece to Red, Gold, Navy, and White and cut out pieces. Remove paper backing.
3. Using a light table, assemble both boats onto the runner and press in place with warm iron.
4. Backstitch the masts with Brown pearl cotton.
5. Follow Finishing instructions on page 82.

Sailboat Table Runner Assembly

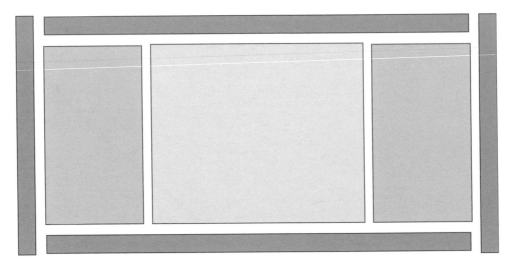

Sand Pail Wall Hanging

photo on page 13
patterns on pages 50 - 52
poem by Sarah Haynes Knoerr

FINISHED SIZE: 21" x 23"
MATERIALS:
½ yard Tan center panel fabric
⅙ yard Navy Blue for inner border
⅓ yard Blue for outer border and binding
⅔ yard White backing fabric
For applique, ¼ yard cuts or scraps of Navy, Gold, Red, White • *DMC* Blue pearl cotton #5 color 311 • Steam-A-Seam II fusible web • Craft & Applique Sheet • Warm & Natural cotton batting

CUTTING:
Cut out Tan Center Block
1   15½" x 18

Cut out Navy Inner Border
2 strips   1½" x 15½" for sides
2 strips   1½" x 20" for top and bottom

Cut out Blue Outer Border
2 strips   2" x 18" for sides
2 strips   2" x 23" for top and bottom

BACKING AND BATTING
1   22" x 24"

BINDING:
Cut 2" strips and sew together for 92"

INSTRUCTIONS:
1. Sew the 1½" x 15½" strips to each side of the center panel.
2. Sew the 1½" x 20" strips to the top and bottom.
3. Sew the 2" x 18" border strips to each side.
4. Sew the 2" x 23" border strips to the top and bottom.
APPLIQUE:

1. Trace all of the applique pieces in reverse onto the fusible web paper using a light table.
2. Using the picture as a color guide, press the traced fusible web pieces to the appropriate fabrics.
3. Cut out shapes.
4. Lay the poem pattern on the light table. Lay the pieced top directly on top so you can see through to the poem.
5. Trace the poem and embroider with pearl cotton using a Backstitch.
6. Peel paper backing off of each piece and lay them directly on top of the pieced top using picture as a guide.
7. Once the pieces are in place, press with iron for 12-14 seconds.
8. Sew the binding pieces together, end to end, to make a continuous strip for binding.
9. Follow Finishing instructions on page 82.

Sand Pail Wall Hanging Assembly

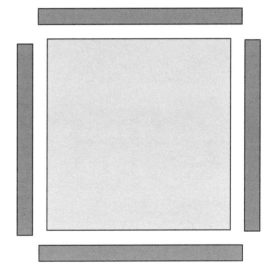

Sand Pail Wall Hanging Outer Border

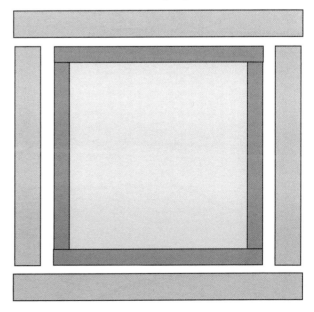

Sand Pail Wall Hanging

photo on page 13
patterns on pages 50 - 52
poem by Sarah Haynes Knoerr

**Words to
Embroider**

**pattern is 100% -
full size**

Sandcastles

Balls and

Children playi

What fun we ha

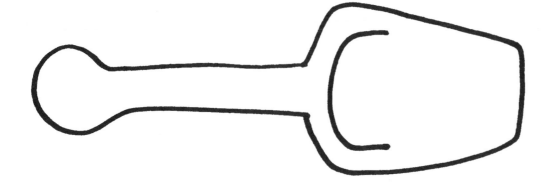

Sand Pail Wall Hanging

photo on page 13
patterns on pages 50 - 52
poem by Sarah Haynes Knoerr

s on the beach

pails galore

ing in the waves

ve at the seashor

shore

Sandcastsles on the beach
Balls and pails galore
Children playing in the waves
What fun we have at the seashore.

Sand Pail Wall Hanging

photo on page 13
patterns on pages 50 - 52

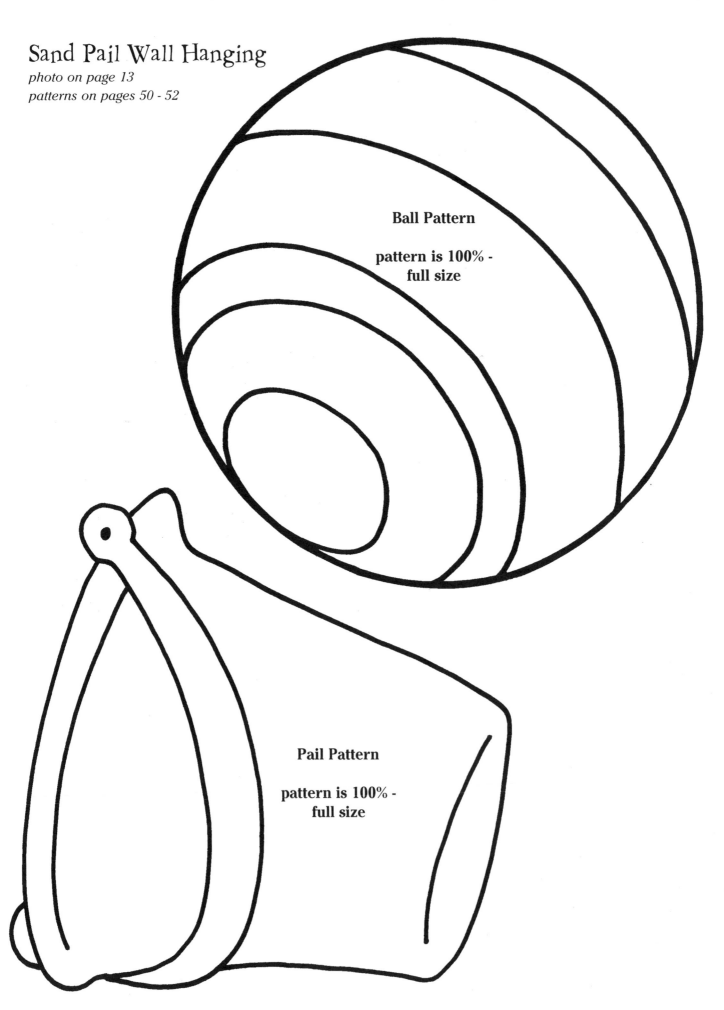

Ball Pattern

pattern is 100% - full size

Pail Pattern

pattern is 100% - full size

Sandcastle Wall Hanging

photo on page 12
patterns on pages 54 - 57
poem by Sarah Haynes Knoerr

Childhood memories of the coast
With all the sounds and smells
Making castles on the beach,
Chasing waves and finding shells.

FINISHED SIZE: 24½" x 24½"

MATERIALS:

½ yard Tan fabric for center panel
⅙ yard Gold fabric for inner border
⅓ yard Seashell print for outer border and binding
¾ yard White fabric for backing
For applique, ¼ yard cuts or scraps of Scraps of 2 shades of Tan, 2 shades of Gold, White, Red • *DMC* Brown pearl cotton #8 Color 433
• Steam-A-Seam II fusible web
• Warm & Natural cotton batting
• Craft & Applique Sheet

CUTTING:

Cut out Tan Center Block
1   18" square

Cut out Gold Inner Border
2 strips   1½" x 18" for sides
2 strips   1½" x 20" for top and bottom

Cut out Shell Print Outer Border
2 strips   2½" x 20" for sides

2 strips   2½" x 24½" for top and bottom

BACKING AND BATTING
1   25" square

BINDING:

Cut 2" strips and sew together for 100"

INSTRUCTIONS:

1. Sew the 1½" x 18" Gold strips to each side of the 18" square.
2. Sew the 1½" x 20" Gold strips to the top and bottom.
3. Sew the 2½" x 20" border strips to each side of the square.
4. Sew the 2½" x 24½" border strips to the top and bottom.

APPLIQUE:

1. Trace all of the applique pieces in reverse onto the fusible web paper using a light table.
2. Using the picture as a color guide, press the traced fusible web pieces to the appropriate fabrics.
3. Cut out shapes.
4. Lay the paper pattern on the ironing board. Lay the Craft & Applique Sheet directly on top so you can see through to the pattern. Peel paper backing off of each sandcastle piece and lay them directly on top of the Craft & Applique Sheet over the pattern. Press for 2-4 seconds. Cool completely.
5. Using a light table, trace the poem onto the wall hanging. Backstitch the words using Brown pearl cotton #433.
6. Peel the sandcastle shape off of the Craft & Applique Sheet and position on the wall hanging.
7. Remove paper backing from the flag, ball, pail, and shovel. Position on wall hanging as shown in photo.
8. Once all of the pieces are in place, press with iron for 12-14 seconds.
9. Using pearl cotton, Backstitch around outline of sandcastle as desired. Backstitch flag pole.
10. Sew the binding pieces together, end to end, to make a continuous strip for binding.
11. Follow Finishing instructions on page 82.

Sandcastle Wall Hanging Center Block

Sandcastle Wall Hanging Outer Border

Sandcastle Wall Hanging

photo on page 12
patterns on pages 54 - 57
poem by Sarah Haynes Knoerr

Words to Embroider
pattern is 100% - full size

Childhood memori

With all the soun

Making castles o

Chasing waves and

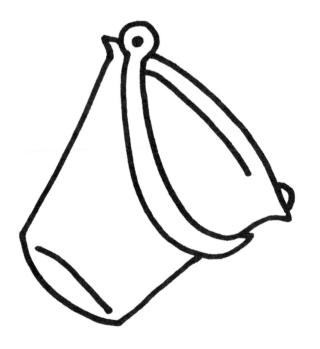

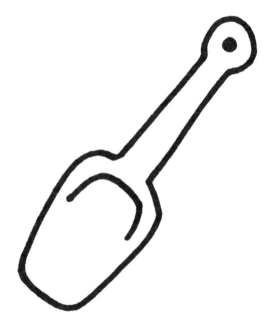

Sandcastle Wall Hanging
photo on page 12
patterns on pages 54 - 57
poem by Sarah Haynes Knoerr

ries of the coast
nds and smells
on the beach,
d finding shells.

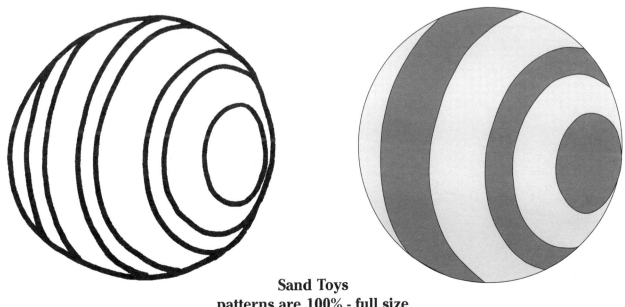

Sand Toys
patterns are 100% - full size

Sandcastle Wall Hanging

photo on page 12
patterns on pages 54 - 57
poem by Sarah Haynes Knoerr

Childhood memories of the coast
With all the sounds and smells
Making castles on the beach,
Chasing waves and finding shells.

**Sandcastle Wall
Hanging**

**pattern is 100% -
full size**

Sandcastle Wall Hanging
photo on page 12
patterns on pages 54 - 57

Ducky Pillow

photo on page 14
patterns on page 59
poem by Sarah Haynes Knoerr

FINISHED SIZE: 13" x 19"
MATERIALS:
⅓ yard Cream color fabric for center panel
⅛ yard Light Purple for corner squares
½ yard Dark Purple fabric for border and backing
For applique, ¼ yard cuts or scraps of Yellow, Orange
• *DMC* Purple pearl cotton #5 • Black pigma pen
• Steam-A-Seam II fusible web • Craft & Applique Sheet
• Warm & Natural cotton batting • Poly-fil stuffing

CUTTING:

Cut out Cream Center Block
1   9½" x 15½"

Cut out Dark Purple Border
2 strips   2½" x 9½" for sides
2 strips   2½" x 15½" for top and bottom

Cut out Light Purple Corners
4   2½" squares

Cut out Dark Purple pillow back
1   13½" x 19½"

Cut out Batting
2   13½" x 19½"

INSTRUCTIONS:

1. Sew the Dark Purple 2½" x 9 strips to each side of the center panel.
2. Sew one 2½" square to each end of the 2½" x 15½" border strips.
3. Sew the Purple strips to the top and bottom of the center panel.

APPLIQUE:

1. Trace all of the applique pieces in reverse onto the fusible web paper using a light table.
2. Using the picture as a color guide, press the traced fusible web pieces to the appropriate fabrics.
3. Cut out shapes.
4. Lay the poem pattern on the light table. Lay the pieced top directly on top so you can see through to the pattern.
5. Trace the poem and embroider with pearl cotton using a Backstitch.
6. Peel paper backing off of each piece and lay them directly on top of the pieced top as shown in photo.
7. Once the pieces are in place, press with iron for 12-14 seconds.
8. Using a Black pigma pen, draw eyes, eyelashes and highlights on the beaks
9. Follow Pillow instructions on page 82.

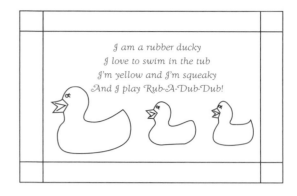

1. Ducky Pillow Center Block and End Borders

2. Ducky Pillow Top and Bottom Borders and End Squares

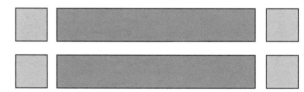

**Words to Embroider
pattern is 100% - full size**

I am a
I love to
I'm yellow
And I play

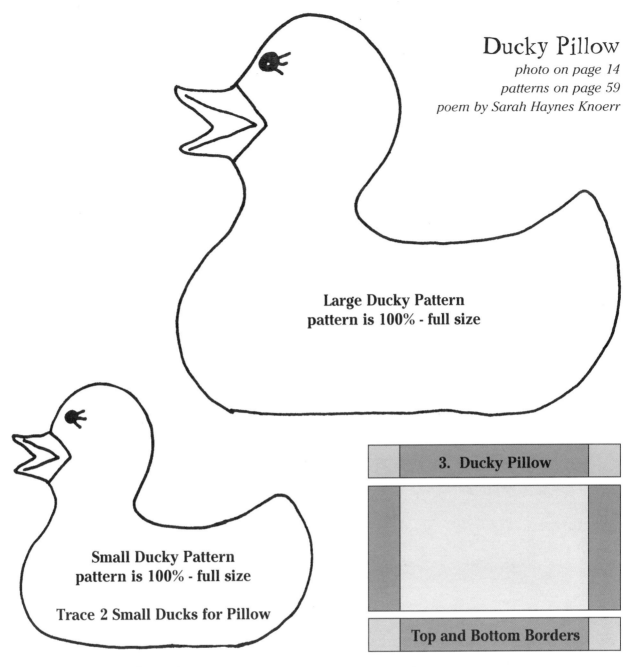

Ducky Pillow
photo on page 14
patterns on page 59
poem by Sarah Haynes Knoerr

Large Ducky Pattern
pattern is 100% - full size

Small Ducky Pattern
pattern is 100% - full size

Trace 2 Small Ducks for Pillow

3. Ducky Pillow

Top and Bottom Borders

a rubber ducky

o swim in the tub

w and I'm squeaky

y Rub-A-Dub-Dub!

Seashell Pillow

photo on page 14
patterns on pages 60 - 61
poem by Gail Kommer

FINISHED SIZE: 13½" x 19"

MATERIALS:

⅓ yard Cream fabric for center panel
⅓ yard Purple fabric for border and backing
For applique, ¼ yard cuts or scraps of Pink, Tan, Brown • *DMC* Purple pearl cotton #5 • Steam-A-Seam II fusible web • Craft & Applique Sheet • Warm & Natural cotton batting • Poly-fil stuffing

CUTTING:

Cut out Cream Center Block
1   10" x 15½"

Cut out Purple Border
2 strips   2½" x 15½" for top and bottom
2 strips   2½" x 14" for sides

Cut out Purple pillow back
1   14" x 19½"

Cut out Batting
2   14" x 19½"

INSTRUCTIONS:

1. Sew the Purple 2½" x 15½" strips to the top and bottom.

2. Sew the Purple 2½" x 14" strips to each side.

APPLIQUE:

1. Trace all of the applique pieces in reverse onto the fusible web paper using a light table.
2. Using the picture as a color guide, press the traced fusible web pieces to the appropriate fabrics.
3. Cut out shapes.
4. Lay the poem pattern on a light table. Lay the pieced top directly on top so you can see through to the pattern.
5. Trace the poem and embroider with pearl cotton using a Backstitch.
6. Peel paper backing off of each piece and lay them directly on top of the pieced top.
7. Once the pieces are in place, press with iron for 12-14 seconds.
8. Follow Pillow instructions on page 82.

Words to Embroider
pattern is 100% - full size

I lift a seashell to n

As along the beach

I listen to the ocean's

Its murmur seems t

Seashell Pillow
photo on page 14
patterns on pages 61 - 63
poem by Gail Kommer

Seashell Patterns

**patterns are 100% -
full size**

Seashell Pillow Assembly Diagram

my ear

ı I walk;

s sounds,

to talk.

She Sells Seashells Wall Hanging

photo on page 14

patterns on pages 62 - 66

Whelk Shells
5 cents

Clam Shells
5 cents

Seashell Sign and Words to Embroider
pattern is 100% - full size

She sells sea

by the seas

Words to Embroider
patterns are 100% - full size

She Sells Seashells
Wall Hanging
photo on page 14
patterns on pages 62 - 66

Scallop Shells
5 cents

Conch Shells
10 cents

Snail Shells
5 cents

:ashells

:shore

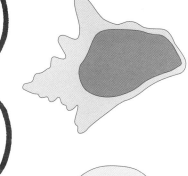

She Sells Seashells Wall Hanging

photo on page 15

patterns on pages 62 - 66

FINISHED SIZE: 23½" x 24½"

MATERIALS:

20" x 21" center panel Blue/Green fabric
⅓ yard Green fabric for border and binding
¾ yard of backing fabric
For applique, ¼ yard cuts or scraps of 2 shades of Tan, Cream, 2 shades of Pink, Gray and Orange • Black pigma pen • Two fabric sheets for inkjet printers (optional) • Steam-A-Seam II fusible web • Craft & Applique Sheet • Warm & Natural cotton batting

CUTTING:

Cut out Blue/Green Center Block
1   20" x 21"

Cut out Green Border
2 strips   2" x 20" for sides
2 strips   2" x 24" for top and bottom

BACKING AND BATTING
1   24" x 25"

BINDING:

Cut 2" strips and sew together for 100"

INSTRUCTIONS:

1. Sew the two 2" x 20" side border strips to the 20" sides of the center panel.
2. Sew the two 2" x 24" border strips to the top and bottom of the panel.
3. Press seams.

APPLIQUE:

1. Using a light table, transfer the words to muslin, using a pigma pen.
    You can also type the words on your computer. Then print the words on computer transfer paper following the manufacturer's directions.
2. Press fusible web to back of muslin.
3. Cut out the signs.
4. Trace all of the applique pieces onto the fusible web paper using the light table.
5. Using the picture as a color guide, press the traced fusible web pieces to the appropriate fabrics.
6. Cut out shapes.
7. Using a pigma pen, draw lines on shells.
8. Peel paper backing off of each piece and position them directly on top of the pieced top as shown in photo.
9. Once the pieces are in place, press with an iron for 12-14 seconds.
10. Follow finishing instructions on page 82.

Seashells Wall Hanging Assembly

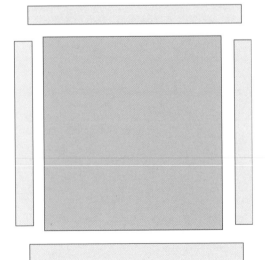

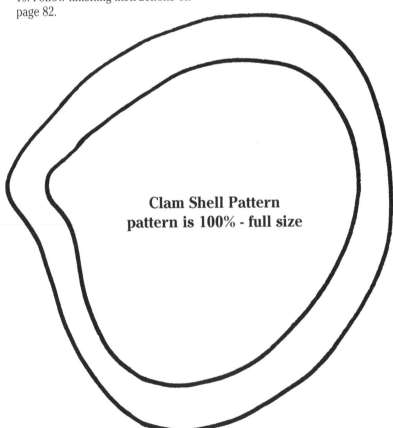

Clam Shell Pattern
pattern is 100% - full size

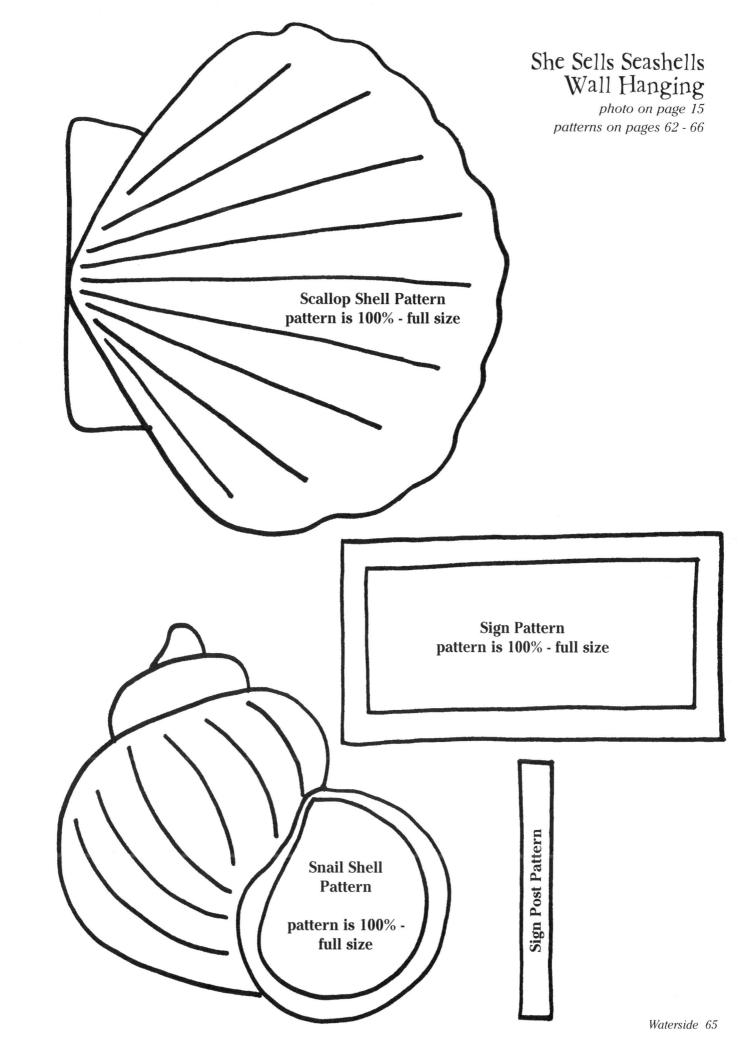

She Sells Seashells
Wall Hanging
photo on page 15
patterns on pages 62 - 66

Scallop Shell Pattern
pattern is 100% - full size

Sign Pattern
pattern is 100% - full size

Snail Shell Pattern

pattern is 100% - full size

Sign Post Pattern

She Sell Seashells Wall Hanging

photo on page 15
patterns on pages 62 - 66

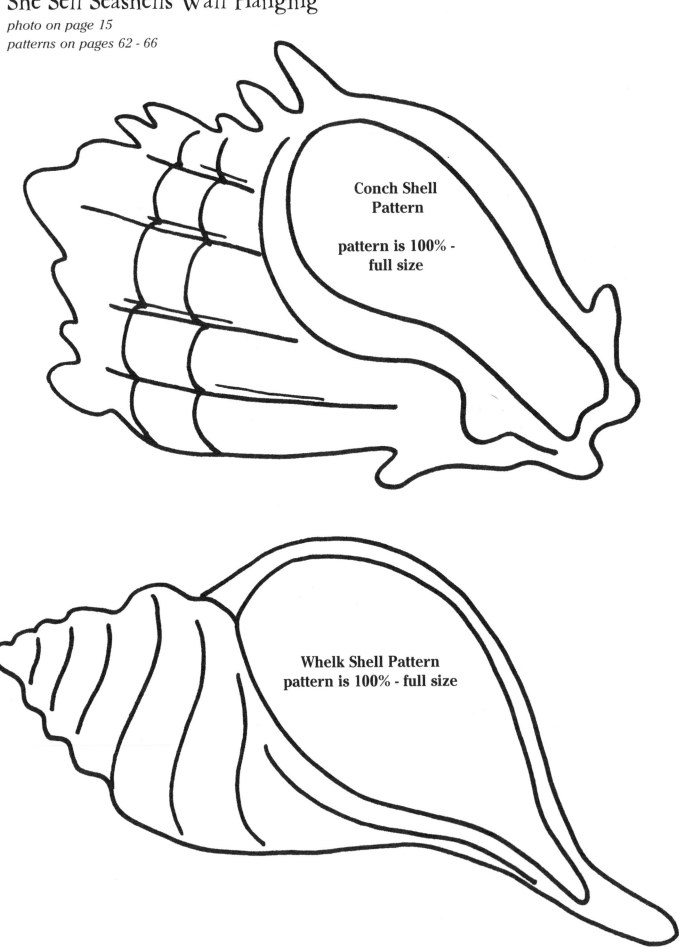

Conch Shell Pattern

pattern is 100% - full size

Whelk Shell Pattern
pattern is 100% - full size

Fish Tales
Wall Hanging

photo on page 16
patterns on pages 67 - 69

Bobber 2 Pattern

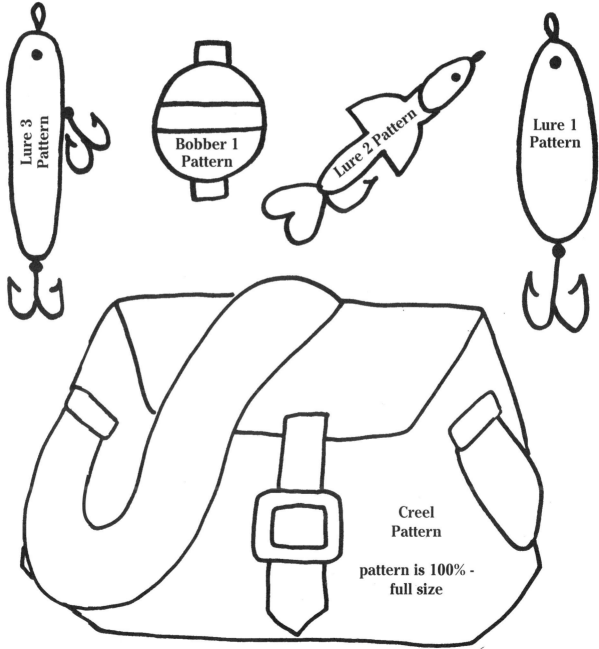

Lure 3 Pattern

Bobber 1 Pattern

Lure 2 Pattern

Lure 1 Pattern

Creel Pattern

pattern is 100% - full size

Fish Tales Wall Hanging

photo on page 16
patterns on pages 67 - 69

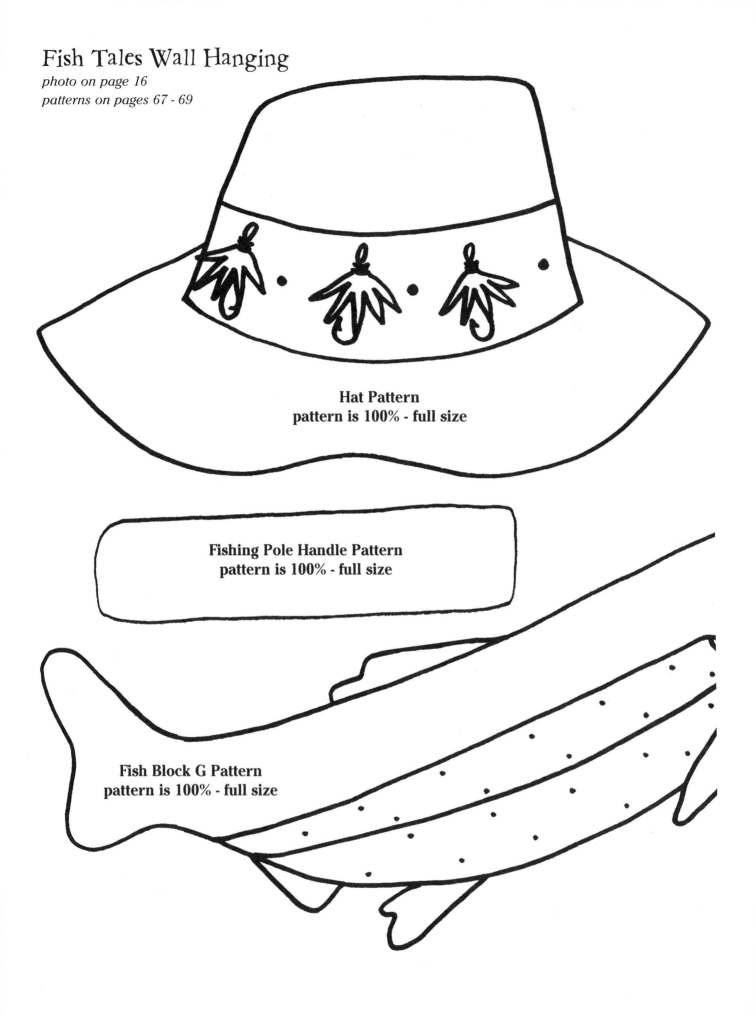

Hat Pattern
pattern is 100% - full size

Fishing Pole Handle Pattern
pattern is 100% - full size

Fish Block G Pattern
pattern is 100% - full size

Fish Tales Wall Hanging

photo on page 16
patterns on pages 67 - 69

Fish Block H Pattern
pattern is 100% - full size

Fish Block A Pattern
pattern is 100% - full size

Fish Tales Wall Hanging

photo on page 16

patterns on pages 67 - 69

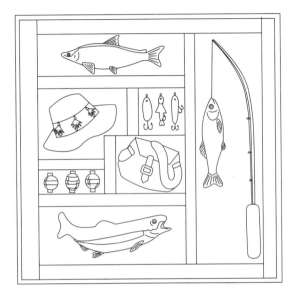

FINISHED SIZE: 25" x 25"

MATERIALS:

⅙ yard Brown sashing fabric

½ yard Brown for border and binding

¾ yard White backing fabric

For applique and blocks, ¼ yard cuts or scraps of 2 shades of Brown, 4 shades of Blue, 4 shades of Tan, Red, Burgundy, White, Muslin, Yellow, Gold, Green, Pink, Black • *DMC* Silver metallic #5 pearl cotton • Black pigma pen • Steam-A-Seam II fusible web • Craft & Applique Sheet • Warm & Natural cotton batting

CUTTING:

Cut out BLOCKS

1   4½" x 13½" from Medium Blue for A

1   4½" x 8½" from Burgundy for C

1   4½" square from Navy Blue for E

1   2½" x 6½" from Burgundy for F

1   2½" x 6½" from Blue for H

1   5½" x 6½" from Tan for J

1   5½" x 13½" from Light Tan for L

1   6½" x 20½" from Light Blue for N

Cut out from Brown fabric for Sashing

2 strips   1½" x 13½" for B and K

1 strip   1½" x 4½" for D

1 strip   1½" x 6½" for G

1 strip   1½" x 5½" for I

1 strip   1½" x 20½" for M

Cut out from Dark Brown fabric for Border

2 strips   2½" x 20½" for sides

2 strips   2½" x 24½" for top and bottom

BACKING AND BATTING

1   25½" square

BINDING:

Cut 2" strips and sew together for 102"

INSTRUCTIONS:

1. Sew a 1½" x 13½" sashing strip B to the bottom of Block A.
2. Sew Block C, Sashing D, and Block E together. Sew this row to the bottom of step 1.
3. Sew Sashing G to the bottom of Block F.
4. Sew Block H to the bottom of Sashing G.
5. Sew Sashing I to the right side of F-G-H.
6. Sew Block J to the right side of Sashing I. Sew this to the bottom of Step 2.
7. Sew Sashing K to the bottom of Step 6.
8. Sew Block L to the bottom of Sashing K.
9. Sew Sashing M to the right side of Step 8.
10. Sew Block N to the right side of Step 9.
11. Sew the 2½" x 20½" borders to each side.
12. Sew the 2½" x 24½" borders to the top and bottom.
13. Press all seams.

Fish Tales Block Assembly

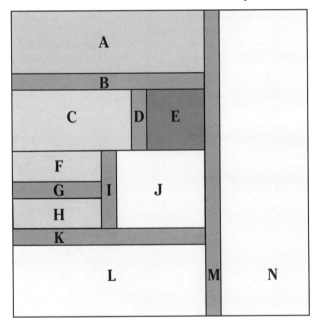

Fish Tales Border Diagram

Fish Tales Wall Hanging

APPLIQUE:

1. Trace all of the applique pieces in reverse onto the fusible web paper using a light table.
2. Using the picture as a color guide, press the traced fusible web pieces to the appropriate fabrics.
3. Draw a line ¼" x 15" and taper the top edge. This is the fishing pole. It will curve in placement. Press to Brown fabric.
4. Cut out shapes.
5. Lay the paper pattern on the ironing board. Lay the Craft & Applique Sheet directly on top so you can see through to the pattern. Peel paper backing off of each piece and lay them directly on top of the Craft & Applique Sheet over the pattern. Press for 2-4 seconds. Cool completely.
6. Using Black pigma pen, draw highlights and eyes on the fish.
7. Peel the shapes off of the Craft & Applique Sheet and position on the wall hanging.
8. Remove paper backing from remaining pieces and position on wall hanging as shown in photo.
9. Press with iron for 12-14 seconds.
10. Using Silver metallic pearl cotton, Backstitch the fishing line and all hooks and loops.
11. Make French knots where dots are shown.
12. Sew the binding pieces together, end to end, to make a continuous strip for binding.
13. Follow the Finishing instructions on page 82.

• •

Down by the Pond Wall Hanging

photo on page 17
patterns on pages 72 - 75

Down by the Pond Border Assembly

FINISHED SIZE: 27" x 27"
MATERIALS:
¾ yard Cream for center panel
½ yard Green polka dot border and binding fabric
1 yard White backing fabric
For applique, ¼ yard cuts or scraps of 2 shades Blue, 2 shades Yellow, 4 shades Brown, 2 shades Tan, 2 shades Green, Black • Black Pigma pen • Steam-A-Seam II fusible web • Craft & Applique Sheet • Warm & Natural cotton batting

CUTTING:

Cut out Light Tan Center panel
1   24" square

Cut out Green Border
2 strips   2" x 24" for sides
2 strips   2" x 27" for top and bottom

BACKING AND BATTING
1   27½" square

BINDING:

Cut 2" strips and sew together for 112"

INSTRUCTIONS:

1. Sew a 2" x 24" border to each side of the center block.
2. Sew a 2" x 27" border to the top and bottom.
3. Press seams.

APPLIQUE:

1. Trace all of the applique piece sin reverse (except pond and cat tails) onto the fusible web paper using a light table.
2. Using the picture as a color guide, press the traced fusible web pieces to the appropriate fabrics.
3. Cut out shapes.
4. Using a light table, draw highlights and eyes with a Black pigma pen.
5. Peel paper backing off of each piece and position them directly on top of the pieced top as shown in photo.
6. Once the pieces are in place, press with iron for 12-14 seconds.
7. Sew the binding pieces together, end to end, to make a continuous strip for binding.
8. Follow Finishing instructions on page 82.

Down by the Pond Wall Hanging

photo on page 17
patterns on pages 72 - 75

Turtle 1 Pattern
pattern is 100% - full size

Down by the Pond Wall Hanging

photo on page 17
patterns on pages 72 - 75

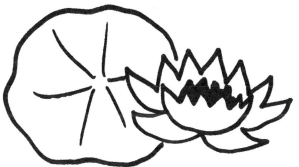

**Lily Pad Patterns
patterns are 100% - full size**

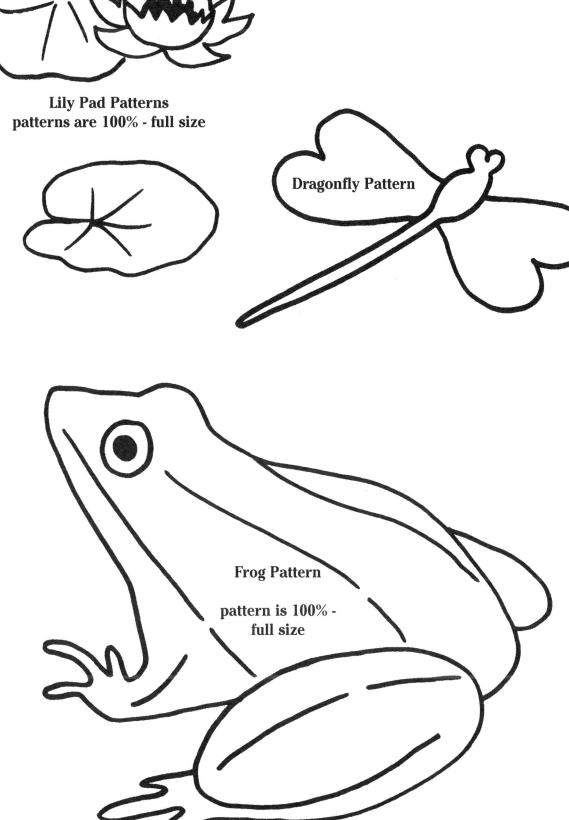

Dragonfly Pattern

Frog Pattern

**pattern is 100% -
full size**

Down by the Pond Hanging

photo on page 17
patterns on pages 72 - 75

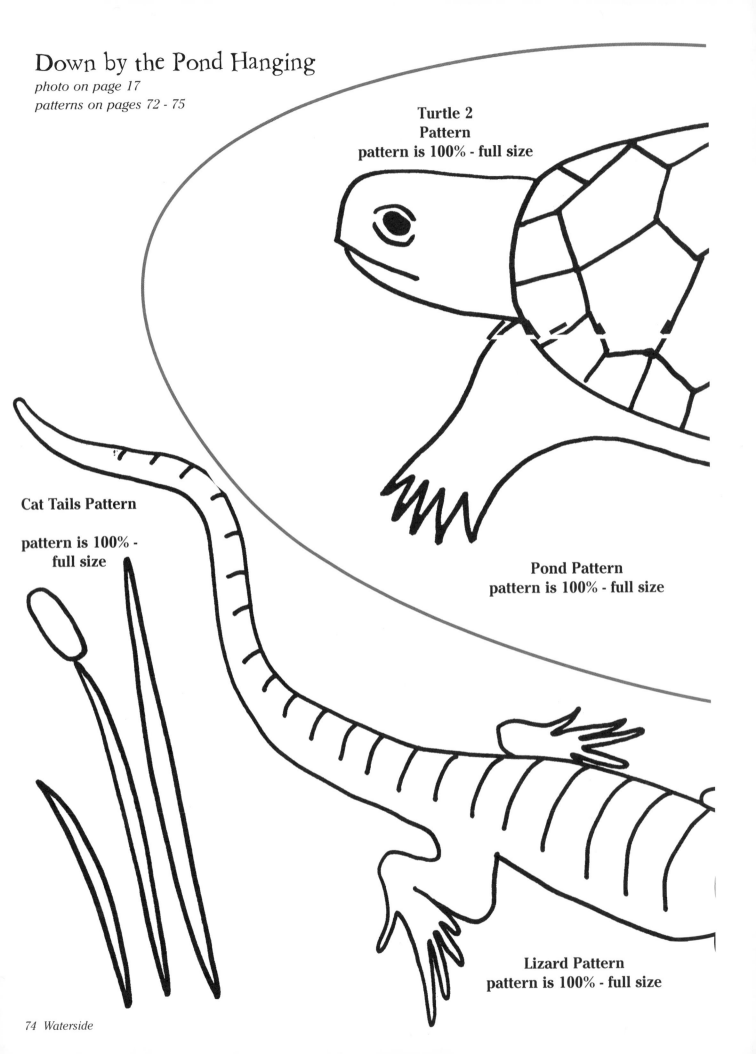

**Turtle 2
Pattern
pattern is 100% - full size**

Cat Tails Pattern

**pattern is 100% -
full size**

**Pond Pattern
pattern is 100% - full size**

**Lizard Pattern
pattern is 100% - full size**

Down by the Pond Wall Hanging
photo on page 17
patterns on pages 72 - 75

Pond Pattern
pattern is 100% - full size

Snail Pattern

pattern is 100% - full size

Under the Sea Wall Hanging

photo on page 83
patterns on pages 78 - 81

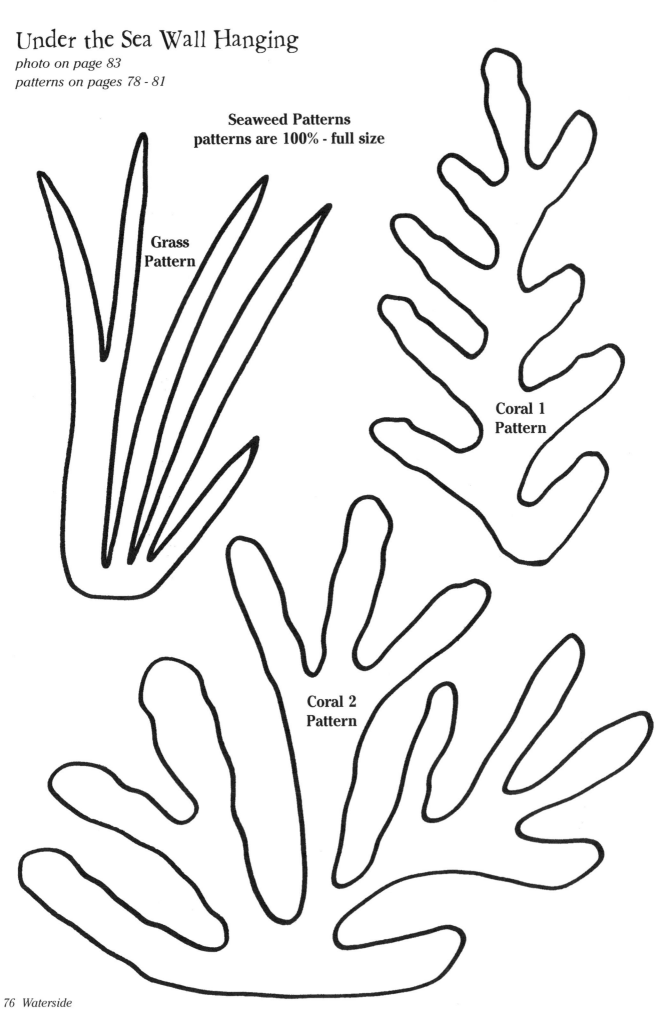

Seaweed Patterns
patterns are 100% - full size

Grass
Pattern

Coral 1
Pattern

Coral 2
Pattern

Under the Sea Wall Hanging

photo on page 83

patterns on pages 78 - 81

FINISHED SIZE:
23½" x 29"

MATERIALS:
⅔ of Blue for center block
½ yard for metallic border
and binding
¾ yard of backing fabric
For applique, ¼ yard cuts or scraps of 2 shades of the following: Cream, Pink/Coral, Orange, Gold, Green, White , Metallic for mermaid tail • Black pigma pen • Steam-A-Seam II fusible web • Craft & Applique Sheet • *Warm & Natural* cotton batting

CUTTING:

Cut out Blue Center Block
1   20" x 25½"

Cut out Metallic Border
2 strips   2" x 23" for sides
2 strips   2" x 28½" for top and bottom

BACKING AND BATTING
1   24" x 30"

BINDING:

Cut 2" strips and sew together for 110"

INSTRUCTIONS:

1. Sew the 2" x 23" borders to the sides.
2. Sew the 2" x 28½" borders to the top and bottom.
3. Press all seams.

APPLIQUE:

1. Trace all of the applique pieces, in reverse, onto the fusible web paper using a light table.
2. Using the picture as a color guide, press the fusible web pieces to the appropriate fabrics.
3. Cut out shapes.
4. Using a light table, draw highlights on fish with a Black pigma pen.
5. Peel paper backing off of each piece and position them directly on top of the pieced top as shown in photo.
6. Once the pieces are in place, press with iron for 12-14 seconds.
7. Follow finishing instructions on page 82.

Under the Sea Border Assembly

Under the Sea Wall Hanging

photo on page 83
patterns on pages 78 - 81

Mermaid Pattern
pattern is 100% - full size

Under the Sea Wall Hanging
photo on page 83
patterns on pages 78 - 81

Under the Sea Wall Hanging

photo on page 83
patterns on pages 78 - 81

**Seaweed and Fish Patterns
patterns are 100% - full size**

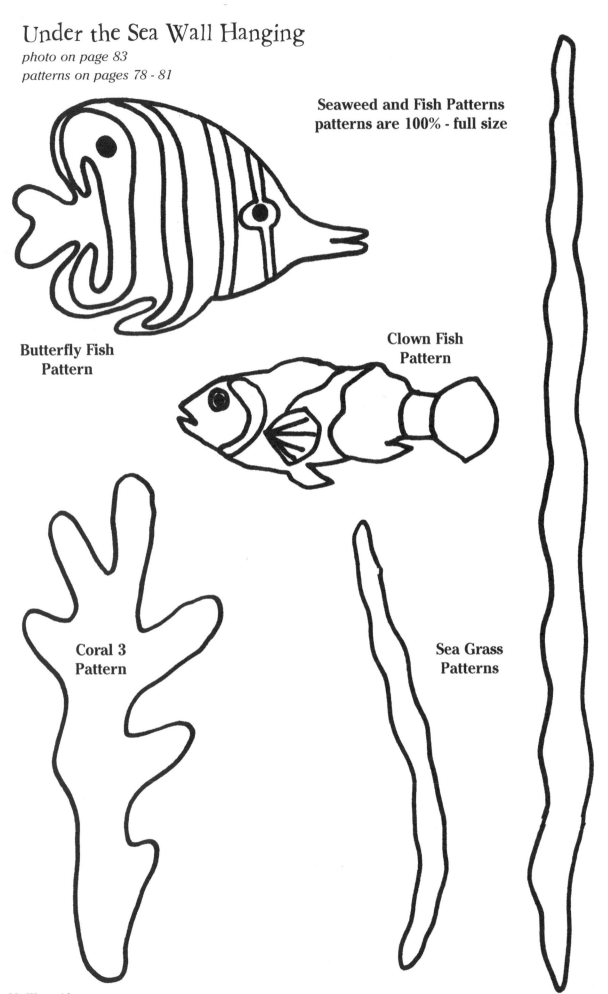

**Butterfly Fish
Pattern**

**Clown Fish
Pattern**

**Coral 3
Pattern**

**Sea Grass
Patterns**